# Moral Thinking, Fast and Slow

In recent research, dual-process theories of cognition have been the primary model for explaining moral judgment and reasoning. These theories understand moral thinking in terms of two separate domains: one deliberate and analytic, the other quick and instinctive.

This book presents a new theory of the philosophy and cognitive science of moral judgment. Hanno Sauer develops and defends an account of "triple-process" moral psychology, arguing that moral thinking and reasoning are only insufficiently understood when described in terms of a quick but intuitive and a slow but rational type of cognition. This approach severely underestimates the importance and impact of dispositions to initiate and engage in critical thinking – the cognitive resource in charge of counteracting myside bias, closed-mindedness, dogmatism, and breakdowns of self-control. Moral cognition is based, not on emotion and reason, but on an integrated network of intuitive, algorithmic, and reflective thinking.

*Moral Thinking, Fast and Slow* will be of great interest to philosophers and students of ethics, philosophy of psychology and cognitive science.

**Hanno Sauer** is Assistant Professor of Ethics at the Department of Philosophy and Religious Studies and a member of the Ethics Institute at Utrecht University, The Netherlands. He is the author of *Moral Judgments as Educated Intuitions* (2017) and *Debunking Arguments in Ethics* (2018).

# Routledge Focus on Philosophy

*Routledge Focus on Philosophy* is an exciting and innovative new series, capturing and disseminating some of the best and most exciting new research in philosophy in short book form. Peer reviewed and at a maximum of fifty thousand words shorter than the typical research monograph, *Routledge Focus on Philosophy* titles are available in both ebook and print on demand format. Tackling big topics in a digestible format, the series opens up important philosophical research for a wider audience, and as such is invaluable reading for the scholar, researcher, and student seeking to keep their finger on the pulse of the discipline. The series also reflects the growing interdisciplinarity within philosophy and will be of interest to those in related disciplines across the humanities and social sciences.

Available:

- **Plant Minds** *Chauncey Maher*
- **The Logic of Commitment** *Gary Chartier*
- **The Passing of Temporal Well-Being** *Ben Bramble*
- **How We Understand Others** *Shannon Spaulding*
- **Political Theory and Global Climate Action** *Idil Boran*
- **Consciousness and Moral Status** *Joshua Shepherd*
- **Knowledge Transmission** *Stephen Wright*
- **Moral Thinking, Fast and Slow** *Hanno Sauer*

For more information about this series, please visit: www.routledge.com/Routledge-Focus-on-Philosophy/book-series/RFP

# Moral Thinking,
# Fast and Slow

**Hanno Sauer**

Routledge
Taylor & Francis Group

LONDON AND NEW YORK

First published 2019
by Routledge
2 Park Square, Milton Park, Abingdon, Oxon OX14 4RN

and by Routledge
605 Third Avenue, New York, NY 10017

First issued in paperback 2020

*Routledge is an imprint of the Taylor & Francis Group, an informa business*

*British Library Cataloguing-in-Publication Data*
A catalogue record for this book is available from the British Library

*Library of Congress Cataloging-in-Publication Data*
Names: Sauer, Hanno, author.
Title: Moral thinking, fast and slow / Hanno Sauer.
Description: 1 [edition]. | New York : Routledge, 2018. | Series:
    Routledge focus on philosophy | Includes bibliographical
    references and index.
Identifiers: LCCN 2018026488 | ISBN 9781138205147
    (hardback : alk. paper) | ISBN 9781315467498 (e-book)
Subjects: LCSH: Judgment (Ethics) | Ethics. | Cognition.
Classification: LCC BJ1408.5 .S385 2018 | DDC 170—dc23
LC record available at https://lccn.loc.gov/2018026488

ISBN 13: 978-0-367-73346-9 (pbk)
ISBN 13: 978-1-138-20514-7 (hbk)

Typeset in Times New Roman
by Apex CoVantage, LLC

I dedicate this book to my brothers,
David and Moritz.

# Contents

# Acknowledgments

The idea for this book goes back to a throwaway remark made by Joseph Heath during a workshop at the University of Toronto's *Centre for Ethics* in 2014 on the theme of Kantian Ethics and Empirical Moral Psychology. I am unable to remember the precise context now, but at one point during his talk Joseph Heath said that in his view, Keith Stanovich's was the most sophisticated and fully developed version of dual process theory he knew of. At the time, I attributed this perception at least in part to friendly collegiality; but when I took a closer look at Stanovich's work, which I had only a cursory familiarity with before, I concluded – as I usually do – that Heath was right. In particular, the idea that cognition is more usefully described in terms of three rather than two fundamental types of processing captured my attention; I found it perfectly compelling, and soon noticed that although there were plenty of dual process theories of moral judgment, a triple process theory of moral cognition had yet to be spelled out. I started wondering how moral judgment and reasoning would look like when described within a triple process framework and – went back to other projects.

Two years later, in early 2016, whilst my wife and I were on parental leave in Llandudno, Cape Town with friends and our and their children, I was contacted by *Routledge* about whether I'd be interested in writing a piece for their new series of short books. And even though I felt flattered, I hesitated at first about whether I wanted to take on such a big project at the time. Then I remembered my "triple process theory of moral judgment," which was a perfect fit for what they seemed to have in mind: much too large a topic for one paper, but perhaps not quite the right size for a research monograph of traditional length. I decided to write up a proposal and signed the contract soon after. I kept collecting ideas, material, literature references and other notes since, but didn't get to writing the bulk of the book before late 2017 in my kitchen in Düsseldorf.

Despite being terse, I found this book difficult to write, mostly due to its essentially essayistic and explorative character. Special thanks thus go to Mark Alfano, Matteo Colombo and Jonathan Webber who read the whole manuscript and provided extremely helpful, thorough, and constructive suggestions for improvement. They have made the book a much, much better one. I want to thank audiences in Bayreuth, Cardiff, and Munich, where I presented some of the material, for their valuable feedback, and to Adam Kolber for letting me write a post about it on his *Neuroethics & Law* blog. I would also like to express my gratitude to Tony Bruce, Adam Johnson and Andrew Weckenmann from *Routledge* for working with me on the book and for their encouragement and professionalism.

# Introduction

Experiments in metaethics are traditionally conducted on the empirically frictionless plane of conceptual analysis (Darwall, Gibbard and Railton 1992). *Début de siècle* ethics is noticeably different: over the past twenty years, philosophers and psychologists have – frequently and fruitfully in tandem – begun to investigate the nature of moral judgment, reasoning, and agency in light of the best contemporary science of the mind. Neuroscience sheds light on which brain areas are involved when subjects contemplate moral dilemmas (Greene 2014); survey studies uncover surprising patterns in people's moral judgments (Knobe 2010); and social psychology demonstrates how fickle and frail our agency is (Doris and Stich 2005, Appiah 2008, Alfano 2016, Tiberius 2014, Sauer 2017b).

In this book, I outline the foundations of an empirically informed theory of moral judgment and reasoning. At the heart of this theory lies the concept of *critical thinking*. I argue that without this concept, moral cognition is only insufficiently understood. With it, new light dawns abruptly over the whole.

This theory is supposed to be both empirically convincing and philosophically satisfying. Over the past two decades, so-called *dual-process theories of cognition* have become the dominant paradigm for understanding moral judgment and reasoning (Greene 2008). Such theories aim to understand moral thinking in terms of two separate mental subsystems: one slow and analytic, the other quick and crude (Kahneman 2011, Evans 2008). Both types of processing suffer from complementary benefits and deficits: one is adaptive and efficient, but prone to error; the other is flexible and sophisticated, but its power is limited, and its deployment costly. However, it has proven surprisingly difficult for dual-process theories of moral judgment to deliver on their main promise of bringing the tools of empirical psychology to bear on the normative questions they originally seemed most interested in.

This book proposes significant revisions and updates to the current cognitive science of moral judgment. I develop and defend a *triple-process account moral psychology*, arguing that moral thinking and reasoning are only poorly understood when described in terms of a quick but intuitive and a slow but controlled type of cognition. This approach severely underestimates the importance and impact of dispositions to initiate and engage in critical thinking – the cognitive resource in charge of initiating intuition override, and of counteracting myside bias, closed-mindedness, dogmatism, breakdowns of self-control, and sheer cognitive laziness. Moral cognition is based, not on emotion or reason or both, but on an integrated network of automatic, algorithmic, and reflective thinking.

Triple-process moral psychology is first and foremost a theory of *intuition override* – how it works and when it is called for. Intuition override is the flipside of critical thinking. Competent moral judgment, especially under modern conditions, crucially depends on subjects' ability to *detect* the need for such override, properly *initiate* it, *monitor* its execution, and *check* its results for accuracy. These four elements of override – detection, initiation, monitoring, and review – are cognitively expensive and affectively unpleasant, which means that only few people tend to engage in them, and only rarely, and only fewer still doing it well. This makes my theory a form of *rationalist pessimism*. I argue that the influence of reason on moral judgment is real and important, but exquisitely difficult and thus rare.

This book has three parts.

In the first, I will briefly explain the basic outlines of dual process accounts in cognitive science and highlight their main claims. I will also zoom in on dual process accounts of *moral* cognition. Here, I will focus on the two richest and most prominent research paradigms within this field, namely *Social Intuitionism* (Haidt 2001) and the aforementioned *Dual Process Model*. I will explain their basic tenets, the main pieces of empirical evidence supporting them, the metaethical and normative conclusions that are supposed to follow from them and their central shortcomings.

In the second part, I will motivate the move towards a triple-process account. I will show that currently existing accounts of moral cognition and reasoning have difficulties explaining, and indeed properly describing, the whens and whys of moral intuition override. I will show that adding a third type of cognitive processing to the mix isn't just semantics. "System III" – or, as I prefer to call it, Type III processing – becomes visible in distinct patterns of breakdown, and its contribution is empirically dissociable from cognitive ability and measurable in terms of individual differences in critical thinking competence. This leads to a *tripartite* model of the architecture of the moral mind. Much of what I do here draws on pioneering recent work in cognitive science (Stanovich 2009a and 2011). This book will be the first to apply this framework to the study of moral judgment.

The third part contains the core of the theory. I will argue that my triple-process theory of moral judgment and reasoning is uniquely equipped to account for moral error as well as breakdowns of moral agency and the conditions under which it is likely to occur. I explore the implications of my theory regarding the shape of moral progress. And I sketch the social and institutional conditions that are required for such progress to become feasible. Here, the upshot of my argument will be at least somewhat bleak, in that modern conditions both uniquely depend on critical moral reflection while, at the same time, being uniquely hostile to its successful deployment. I thus consider whether, at the level of theory, we may have to become *elitists* about moral judgment, suggesting that, due to the inherent difficulty of critical thinking and the associated costs of doing it badly, moral judgment is something the vast majority of people should simply refrain from.

Ultimately, my goal is to explore the normative implications of this model. So far, many authors have tried to show that the evidence from cognitive science doesn't support a vindication of consequentialist morality (Berker 2009, Sauer 2012a, Kahane et al. 2015). Very few people, however, have tried to develop a constructive alternative. This is what my ultimate aim is here. I wish to show which set of moral beliefs is recommended by the triple-process account of moral judgment developed here.

The normative conclusions following from my account are unapologetically progressive. I argue that the triple-process account of moral judgment and reasoning strongly supports the superiority of a particular type of moral and political outlook – one that emphasizes the need for open-mindedness, resistance to dogmatism, an inclusive attitude and a constant revision of the ways of living with one another bequeathed to us by previous generations. It does so on the basis of the epistemic superiority of the cognitive processes that yield such an outlook at the expense of intuitively appealing and emotionally compelling but frequently foolish and harmful moral-political views.

# 1 Dual process theory

## Dual process theory: origins

The idea that the mind is functionally differentiated is not new. But after spending quite some time in hiding under the name of "faculty psychology" as one of philosophy's many – *many* – shameful family secrets, it experienced a threefold revival in the final quarter of the 20th century, with psychology, economics, and philosophy for once converging on something. Nowadays, the name "two systems" or "dual process" theory has become common parlance. Its heyday culminated in the so-called Nobel Prize for Economics in 2002 and was closely followed, as if to grimly confirm its central predictions, by the inception of postalethic politics. No doubt when people first came up with the distinction between System I and System II, they did not expect that political parties would feel compelled to pick sides.

In *psychology*, many of the central insights of dual process theory were anticipated by studies showing how easily human judgment and agency is swayed by extraneous features of the situation, how prone people are to confabulation (Nisbett and Wilson 1977 and 1978, Hirstein 2005) and how much of their thinking goes on beneath the tip of the cognitive iceberg (Wilson 2002). Many of our intuitive judgments don't hold up under closer scrutiny. And the errors we make aren't just random, either: people's thinking follows predictable patterns of error.[1]

Much of the work leading to dual process psychology has thus been about devising clever ways to trick people into revealing how feeble-minded they are. In *behavioral economics*, this art was perfected by Amos Tversky and Daniel Kahneman (1982; see also Kahneman 2003), who were able to show in just how many ways human beings deviate from standard models of rational choice. Though not originally the focal point of their work, Kahneman (2000) subsequently confirmed that "Tversky and I always thought of the heuristics and biases approach as a two-process theory" (682). Later, Kahneman would go on to write the instant classic *Thinking, Fast and Slow*, the title of which is plagiarized by this book.

For some reason, people stubbornly refuse to adhere to the norms of reasoning and decision-making postulated by economists. This is not to indict these norms as invalid; but as far as their descriptive adequacy is concerned, Kahneman and Tversky were able to show that they belong squarely in the Platonic realm. Take statistics and probability, for instance. People routinely confuse what is most likely with what they can most easily recall examples of (this is called the *availability heuristic*, Tversky and Kahneman 1973). Depending on context, they think that there are cases in which A + B is more likely than A (this is called the *conjunction fallacy*). And virtually everyone prefers driving to flying, which at least keeps the undertakers employed (Sunstein 2005a).

Many of Kahneman and Tversky's insights were modeled in terms of their *prospect theory* (Kahneman 2003, 703ff.), according to which people's utility function is an S-shaped curve, with a subtle kink in the origin. This entails that, unlike what is assumed in standard rational choice theory, both gains and losses have diminishing utility, and that losses hurt more. The first theorem is particularly striking. Think about it: if utility diminishes as it increases, how *could* disutility diminish as well? It's hard to make sense of, until one accepts that what matters to people isn't amounts of, but *changes* in utility. At (roughly) the same time, Richard Thaler conducted his first studies on the *endowment effect* (1980; see also Thaler 2015, 12ff.). He, too, found that people intuitively disvalue losses more than they value gains.

These mistakes are much like optical illusions. Even when their flaws are exposed, they remain compellingly misleading. But the interesting thing about them is that their flaws *can* be exposed: when the true answer to a question or the correct solution to a problem is pointed out to them, even laypeople often recognize that their intuition led them astray. This suggests that people are capable of two types of information processing, one swiftly yielding shoddy judgments on the basis of quick-and-dirty rules of thumb, the other occasionally yielding correct judgments on the basis of careful analytic thinking. Keith Stanovich came up with the deliberately non-descriptive System I/System II terminology to capture this distinction whilst avoiding the historical baggage of concepts such as "reason" or "intuition."

Finally, *philosophy* made its own contribution, perhaps best exemplified by Jerry Fodor's (1983) groundbreaking work on the "modularity of mind." Though not strictly speaking *Team Two Systems*, Fodor argued that the mind comprises a surprisingly large amount of domain-specific modules that frequently carry out one, and only one, specific task, such as facial recognition or guessing the trajectory of falling objects. Fodor identified the following nine characteristics that give a type of processing a claim to modularity:

- domain-specificity
- mandatory operation
- limited accessibility
- quickness
- informational encapsulation
- simple outputs
- specific neural architecture
- characteristic patterns of breakdown
- characteristic pattern of ontogenetic development (38ff.)

System I processes are frequently dedicated to very specific functions, operate on the basis of shallow, inflexible rules and are neither consciously accessible (just *how* are you able to recognize your mother out of the 100 billion people that have ever lived?) nor cognitively penetrable. The good news is that they require virtually no effort, and can easily run in parallel.

The list of things we are bad at is ineffably long, and includes general domains such as probability, logic, exponential reasoning, large numbers and gauging risks as well as more specific bugs such as hindsight bias, confirmation bias, anchoring effects, framing effects, and so on. In all of these cases, System I routinely comes up with intuitively compelling but demonstrably incorrect pseudo solutions to a variety of problems. Most of the aforementioned authors are thus strongly in favor of relying on System II as much as possible.

System I and II processes can be distinguished along several dimensions: popular criteria for discriminating between intuitive and non-intuitive thinking have to do with whether an episode of information processing is automatic or controlled, quick or slow, perceptual or

*Table 1.1* Features of Systems I & II: Four Clusters (adapted from Evans 2008, 257)

| System I | System II |
|---|---|
| **Cluster I (Consciousness)** | |
| Unconscious | Conscious |
| Implicit | Explicit |
| Automatic | Controlled |
| Low effort | High effort |
| Rapid | Slow |
| High capacity | Low capacity |
| Default process | Inhibitory |
| Holistic, perceptual | Analytic, reflective |
| **Cluster II (Evolution)** | |
| Old | Recent |
| Evolutionary rationality | Individual rationality |
| Shared with animals | Uniquely human |
| Nonverbal | Language-dependent |
| Modular | Fluid |
| **Cluster III (Functionality)** | |
| Associative | Rule-based |
| Domain-general | Domain-specific |
| Contextualized | Abstract |
| Pragmatic | Logical |
| Parallel | Sequential |
| **Cluster IV (Individual differences)** | |
| Universal | Heritable |
| Independent of general intelligence | Linked to general intelligence |
| Independent of working memory | Limited by working memory capacity |

analytic, and so forth. It is useful to sort these features into four main "clusters" (Evans 2008, 257) (see Table 1.1).

System I and II processes differ with regard to whether they require conscious control and draw on working memory (cluster 1), how evolutionarily old they are (cluster 2), whether they are implemented through symbolic, frequently language-based thought (cluster 3) and whether one can find strong across-the-board individual differences between them (cluster 4).

This leads to a straightforward account of the architecture of the mind according to which there are two basic types of information processing (see Figure 1.1).

How these two types of processing relate to each other and whether this account is sufficiently rich is the topic of this book. I will argue, perhaps unsurprisingly, that it is not.

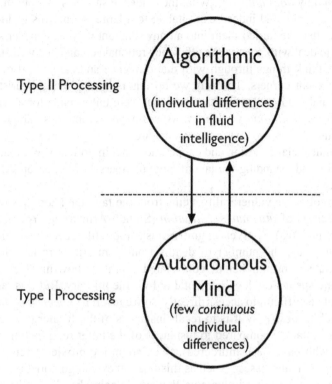

Type II Processing

Type I Processing

*Figure 1.1* Two Systems (adapted from Stanovich 2011, 122)

System I has an essentially economic rationale: it is about saving expensive and scarce cognitive resources. Through training and exercise, the mind is generally very good at allowing tasks that at first require effortful System II thinking to migrate into System I. When this happens, conscious thinking becomes intuitive via *habituation*. The modularity of the mind is essentially due to the same process, but on a phylogenetic level: mental modules that carry out important domain-specific tasks are evolutionarily accumulated cognitive capital. System II, then, has enabled us to create a specific niche for a *Mängelwesen* like us to thrive by supplementing the fossilized wisdom of previous generations with a flexible problem-solving mechanism preparing us for the unexpected.

Dual process theorists relish our cognitive shortcomings, but it would be misleading, or at the very least an overstatement, to suggest that our mind simply *does not work*. What the evidence shows is that our minds are vulnerable, and indeed exploitable; to a large extent, this is due to the fact that we hurled them into an environment they were never supposed to deal with. System I's efficiency rationale entails that we cannot always think things through with due diligence and care. Most of the time, we cut corners. The way we do this is by deploying heuristics, rough-and-ready cognitive shortcuts that were tailor-made for an *environment of evolutionary adaptedness* we no longer inhabit: small groups of around 150 people whose members are strongly genetically related, with tight social cohesion and cooperation and, importantly, without the need for understanding the law of large numbers or the diamond/water paradox.

Our cognitive vulnerability stems from the fact that heuristics work on the basis of *attribute substitution* (Sinnott-Armstrong, Young and Cushman 2010). A given cognitive task implicitly specifies a *target attribute*, say, the number of deaths from domestic terrorist attacks per year vs. the number of gun-related deaths or how much money the state spends on developmental aid vs. the military. But this target attribute is difficult to access directly, so we resort to a *heuristic attribute* such as how easy it is to recall instances of the former (domestic terrorist attacks) compared to instances of the latter (e. g. people you know who have been murdered). Such cognitive proxies often work fine, but in many cases – such as this one – they can go horribly awry, and prompt intuitive judgments that are hopelessly off. In the case of moral judgment, people sometimes seem to substitute "emotionally revolts me" for "is morally wrong" (Schnall et al. 2008; see also Slovic et al. 2002) – with disastrous effects.[2]

But not everyone is this pessimistic about intuition. Some authors insist that our mind's proneness to error is essentially an artifact created by overzealous trappers hell-bent on finding flaws in our thinking by exposing unsuspecting participants to ecologically invalid toy problems (Gigerenzer 2008), that is, psychologists. In real-world contexts, on the other hand, relying on intuition is not just inevitable, but frequently constitutes the most adaptive trade-off between efficiency and accuracy (Wilson 2002).

To a certain extent, friends and foes of System I are talking past each other. Some argue that System I performs well under ecologically valid conditions; some show that it performs badly when confronted with novel or unusual tasks. These two claims are only rhetorically at odds with each other, and reflect differences in emphasis more than in substance.

The evolutionary origins of our mind explain another of its important features, which is its essentially *inhibitive* character. There is a kernel of truth in sensationalist claptrap such as the claim that our skulls house a "lizard brain," which is that unlike an intelligent designer, evolution does not go back to the drawing board (Hirstein 2005, 31; Heath 2014a, 45). Instead, it builds new structures on top of old ones, which means that frequently, the newer structures have little else to do but monitor and selectively disinhibit their unruly forbearers.

Pathological phenomena such as confabulation or utilization behaviors (Wegner 2002, Schlosser 2012) suggest that this may be how action works in general. The experience of action initiation that starts from a prior state of mental inaction is essentially the opposite of the truth, which is that the mind is in a constant state of being prepared to seize upon various affordances in its immediate surroundings that needs to be suppressed and only released when appropriate. The relationship between System I and higher cognitive processes is thus essentially one of *default interventionism* in which conscious reflection has to figure out whether, when, and how to interfere with the stream of intuitions it is being fed.

A final thing I would like to mention to lay some ground for what follows is how many of the features of System II are rife with moral content. Non-intuitive processing is in charge of

> the tendency to collect information before making up one's mind, the tendency to seek various points of view before coming to a conclusion, the disposition to think extensively about a problem before responding, the tendency to calibrate the degree of strength of one's opinion to the degree of evidence available, the tendency to think about future consequences before taking action, the tendency to explicitly weigh pluses and minuses of situations before making a decision, and the tendency to seek nuance and avoid absolutism.
>
> (Stanovich 2011, 36)

Moreover,

> the decontextualizing demands of modernity increasingly require such characteristics as: fairness, rule-following despite context, even-handedness, nepotism prohibitions, unbiasedness, universalism, inclusiveness, contractually mandated equal treatment, and

discouragement of familial, racial, and religious discrimination. These requirements are difficult ones probably for the reason that they override processing defaults related to the self.

(76)

All of these features, I suggest, are not just epistemically, but *morally* different from the seductive appeal of one's gut feelings and call-it-like-I-see-it idiocy.

## Dual process theory: prospects and perils

Dual process theories suffer from various problems and limitations, some empirical, some conceptual (see Evans and Stanovich 2013 for the following discussion). It should be noted that talk of "systems" is already misleading, because it suggests that there really are distinct, identifiable, and perhaps neurally separate systems in charge of intuitive and non-intuitive thinking. This is not the case. A distinction between different *types* of cognition better captures the fact that intuitive and non-intuitive thinking refer to different modes of cognition, rather than distinct mental faculties. I therefore prefer to speak of Type I- and Type II processing, though I will also frequently use the more common Systems terminology for reasons of simplicity and to avoid repetitiveness.

Talk of *two* systems misleads even further, because it suggest that there is a specific number of systems, and that that number is two. This could not be further from the truth. In fact, System I is a hodgepodge of many different subsystems, modules, cognitive scripts and types of processing, all lumped together to highlight certain aspects that they share. System II, despite the fact that, as I will argue, it needs to be further differentiated in algorithmic Type II processing and reflective Type III processing, also consists of a variety of modes of thinking, ranging from logical inference to story-telling to explanatory reasoning. Stanovich thus recently abandoned his own System I/System II distinction, now referring to System I as TASS (*the autonomous set of systems*) to highlight its disunified, cluster-like structure.

Leaving issues of appropriate labeling aside, dual process accounts are also plagued by more substantive problems. Firstly, the features characteristic of the two types of processing identified above sometimes cross-cut. For instance, not all automatic processes are evolutionarily old. Facial recognition may be, but intuitively making a skilled chess move is not. Likewise, not all intuitive judgments are biased. Conscious reflection can generate normatively inferior responses. And finally, not all affective processes are rapid. Grief, for instance, takes time. However, this problem is to a certain extent an artifact resulting from the way in which the features of Type I and Type II processing are typically presented. Figure 1.1 above, for instance, makes it seem as if the listed properties necessarily had to co-occur such that if they did not, dual process theory would be refuted. However, dual process theorists can easily admit that these features are merely robustly correlated, and should not be misunderstood as essential properties.

Secondly, cognitive processing is continuous rather than discrete. Some processes are more System I-ish, some more System II-ish, and very few exclusively belong to one of the two. Virtually all processes of judgment formation will contain intuitive as well as controlled elements of cognition. Critical, reflective thinking can be triggered by an implicit sense of unease; feelings of revulsion can result from careful consideration of an issue. However, this, too, poses a fundamental problem for dual process accounts only if one takes them to be committed to the idea that for the distinction between Type I and II to make sense, this distinction must refer to discrete entities. But this is a commitment dual process theorists can easily drop, acknowledging that their terminology picks out ideal types of processing which are located on a spectrum of more hybrid types.

Thirdly, it is sometimes suggested that the accumulated data can be accounted for within a computational single-process framework (Kruglanski and Gigerenzer 2011). Partly, this claim is also a semantic one: in a sense, it's all one thing, namely *cognition*. But this suggestion skips the issue of whether the Type I/Type II/Type III distinction provides an analytically useful and explanatorily fruitful general framework for understanding cognition. Moreover, it is based on the false allegation that dual process theorists deny that Type I operations are rule-based, which they do not and need not.

Fourth, the multiple systems framework is empirically extremely well-supported. Evidence from neuroscientific findings, cognitive load studies, research into cognitive styles and individual differences, lesion studies, emotional manipulation or neuromodulators all converge on the suggestion that the mind processes information in (at least) two fundamentally different ways – one frugal but hit-and-miss, one costly but mostly on target.

Let me be clear, however, that I do agree with the critics in that I think current dual process models of human cognition leave a lot of room for improvement. The psychology of moral cognition and reasoning in particular would benefit greatly from moving towards a triple-process framework. To spell this out is the focus of this book. But before I motivate this move, let me briefly explain how "two system" accounts found their way into the psychology of moral cognition and reasoning, and how they have shaped the field of empirically informed metaethics.

## Dual process theory: moral judgment

Dual process theories in the cognitive science of moral judgment come in three forms: there are cooperative, competitive, and servile accounts. I will take them up in reverse order.

Servile accounts echo Hume in claiming reason to be the slave of the passions. Worse still, it is a deluded slave who deems himself to be the master. According to such accounts, individual moral reasoning typically neither produces nor changes people's moral beliefs. Rather, their beliefs are formed on an intuitive level. Conscious justifications only kick in after the fact, and when they do, it is to rationalize whatever judgment a subject has already arrived at. Various metaphors have been proposed for this, such as that of a rational but largely powerless rider and an emotional but largely dominant elephant (Haidt 2012), an emotional dog wagging its rational tail (Haidt 2001) or, perhaps somewhat tendentiously, that of a lawyer arguing a predetermined case for a client rather than a scientist impartially pursuing the truth.

This metaphor is most richly spelled out by the *Social Intuitionist* model of moral judgment (Haidt and Björklund 2008) (see Figure 1.2).

According to this model, conscious reasoning rarely directly produces moral judgments; rather, moral reasoning is typically in the business of justifying spontaneously and non-inferentially formed moral intuitions. In many cases, this will not amount to much more than simple rationalization; in some cases, reasoning may in fact be nothing but confabulation, such as when subjects try to justify their moral intuitions in terms of considerations that demonstrably do not apply to a given case.

Various types of evidence support this model. One comes from the alacrity of moral judgment. Moral judgments are made rapidly. Another

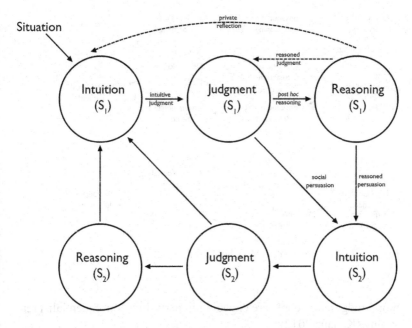

*Figure 1.2* The *Social Intuitionist* Model (adapted from Haidt 2001)

comes from the imperviousness of moral intuition. (I will discuss the fascinating phenomenon of "moral dumbfounding" below.) A third is due to the complete disconnect between moral beliefs and moral reasoning that can sometimes be observed. In cases of moral choice blindness, subjects can be induced to endorse moral judgment, and provide justifications for them, which are inconsistent with what they previously professed (Hall, Johansson and Strandberg 2012).

Competitive accounts such as the dual process model paint a more bellicose picture of how moral cognition works (see Figure 1.3). The dual process model is neither exclusively rationalist nor intuitionist (in the optional anti-rationalist sense), but adopts each account selectively depending on which type of moral judgment is put under the microscope (or brain scanner, for that matter). It starts out from a distinction between characteristically deontological and characteristically consequentialist moral judgments. This is a clever move or a cheap trick – depending on one's loyalties to one or the other camp – because it is actually highly implausible that in arriving at their characteristically consequentialist

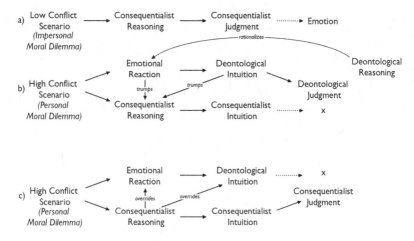

*Figure 1.3* The *Dual Process* Model of Moral Cognition

moral judgment, people are engaging in party-line consequentialist reasoning (Kahane 2012).

The way these rough types of moral judgment are operationalized is via a series of famous philosophical thought experiments such as *Trolley* and *Footbridge* cases.[3]

In previous work I criticized Greene (Sauer 2012a) for his attempt to provide a neuroscientific vindication of consequentialist moral beliefs, though I now think this criticism is only partly correct, and that the issue trades almost entirely on the bullet-biting/intuition chasing distinction (Greene 2014). This, however, is a distinction *within types of moral reasoning* – rationalization vs. following the argument where it leads – rather than an attempt to undermine the normative force of deontological intuitions on the basis of the System I/System II distinction. And it seems clear anyway that neuroscience as such can play virtually no role in deciding whether a given type of reasoning should count as genuine or confabulatory.

One interesting recent development in this debate has to do with moral learning (Nichols et al. 2016, Railton 2017) and the ameliorative effects it can have on people's moral intuitions. However, Greene (2017) seems to me largely right in stressing the fact that for a number of pressing problems characteristic of modern societies, the prospects of moral learning are dim. The training processes successfully attuning people's moral intuitions to the normative infrastructure of everyday morality are either ineffective or counterproductive when it comes to appreciating the intricacies of global politics, modern technology, or the spontaneous order of the market. For the same reason – their inadequacy in dealing with far-fetched toy problems (see Sauer 2018, chapter 6) – I find Greene's sweeping (though perhaps no longer all-encompassing) rejection of deontological intuitions unimpressive, because this rejection remains restricted to the use of moral intuitions about unecological cases.

Cooperative theories such as the Educated Intuitions account (Sauer 2017a) emphasize how System I and II work together to produce moral judgments. Emotionally charged dispositions provide the raw material, moral reasoning figures in the acquisition, formation, maintenance, and reflective correction – in short: education – of moral intuitions on the basis of this raw material. People's educated intuitions then constitute the basis for episodes of moral reasoning, which are responses to socially entertained challenges. This challenge-and-response process creates feedback loops into people's intuitions, thereby educating them further (see Figure 1.4).

Importantly, the Educated Intuitions account explains why there is, at least in principle, nothing dubious about the intuitive character of moral judgment, the *post hoc* nature of moral justification, or the social function of moral reasoning. In addition to the economic rationale of saving expensive cognitive resources, virtually all automatic cognitive patterns show some degree of overlearning, which consists in a

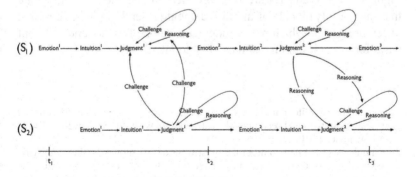

*Figure 1.4* The *Educated Intuitions* Model

migration of higher-order cognitive processes into intuitive streams of judgment formation. These habitualized intuitions are the hinges on which the doors of moral justification turn. Moral reasoning typically comes after the fact, then, because it doesn't consist in unprompted and gratuitous cognitive labor, but in responding to specific challenges put forward against one's moral intuitions. It is then not particularly damning to find that people do not drop their moral beliefs like hot potatoes when they encounter possible challenges. It seems prima facie rational to defend one's beliefs at least to some extent, and within reasonable limits. Finally, it is eminently useful to socially distribute the burdens of moral justification. Moral reasoning, like other forms of reasoning, has an adversarial structure in which various cognitive dispositions that look like bugs at an individual level turn out to be features when viewed from a socially extended perspective. Moral reasoning is a collaborative enterprise in which multiple individuals' educated moral intuitions interlock to push the frontier of moral knowledge forward and leave a trail of moral error behind.

It would be misleading to suggest that servile, competitive, and cooperative accounts of moral judgment and reasoning are deeply incompatible with each other. It is probably more accurate to see these models as emphasizing and highlighting different aspects of moral cognition; neither theory denies that the other two describe some, or perhaps even many, instances of moral judgment and episodes of moral reasoning correctly. Social Intuitionists do not deny that reasoning sometimes feeds back into our moral intuitionist to educate them; dual process theorists do not deny that System I and II sometimes work together. The most accurate representation of moral judgment would thus be one where Figures 1.2, 1.3, and 1.4 are *superimposed* on one another to illustrate that the various models of moral judgment currently on offer describe different ways in which moral judgments can be formed, and different ways for moral intuition and reasoning to interact.

## Notes

1  The dual process literature is vast, so I cannot reference all of it here. For useful critical introductions, I recommend Evans and Frankish (2009) as well as Evans and Stanovich (2013).
2  It should be noted that some of the most well-known studies on the amplifying power of disgust on moral judgment have failed to replicate. In other cases, the findings reported in the literature are likely attributable to publication bias. For more on these issues, see Landy and Goodwin (2015). At any rate, even if they did replicate and even if there were no publication bias, effect sizes would be small and restricted to remain certain subgroups of the population (May 2014).

3 The Trolley and Footbridge cases are so-called sacrificial dilemmas which are heavily used in the empirical study of moral judgment. Typically, they involve a runaway trolley threatening to kill a group of individuals and the question whether, and how, a single individual may or may not be sacrificed to prevent the death of the larger group. See, for instance, Kahane et al. (2015).

# 2 From dual to triple process theory

## Motivating triple process theory

The main distinction that I wish to spell out in this book is the one between Type II and Type III processing. What reasons are there to adopt it? What's wrong with simply sticking to our beloved categories of fast and slow thinking? There are three main reasons for joining the (incipient) movement.

For one thing, the difference between Types I, II, and III manifests in different *patterns of breakdown*. Different things happen, and different deficits result, when the respective types of processing become impaired. Stanovich notes that impairments of System I typically yield highly specific modular deficiencies. People with prosopagnosia, for instance, have difficulty recognizing faces; individuals on the Autism spectrum show atypical social cognition; lesion patients have difficulties with practical reasoning (the locus classicus here is Damasio 1994).

These System I defects show very few, if any, continuous individual differences. No one is generally bad at automatic cognition across the board. From the fact that one person isn't very good at remembering or recognizing faces, we can conclude almost nothing about how they will do with regard to "the rest" of their System I. That's because, as we've already noted earlier, there is no monolithic rest: the term System I is even more of an artificial catch-all than the others. System I is simply a collection of essentially independent genres of cognition whose performance is fairly disconnected.

System II impairments, on the other hand, manifest in what is commonly referred to as "mental retardation." Low cognitive ability results in lower intelligence scores and visible deficits in abstract or spatial reasoning of the kind measured by intelligence tests (Stanovich 2009b). These deficits are unspecific: System II houses raw processing power, with little or no regard to how that power is used. This also means that impairments of Type II processing can make a difference to people's memory, reasoning, planning, and other abilities.

Breakdowns of Type III processing, then, do not manifest in lower cognitive ability per se. Rather, when Type III processing is impaired, people's *critical thinking* breaks down, while their ability to engage in conscious reasoning frequently remains intact. Symptomatic for this are cognitive delusions in which people are often busy constructing demonstrably inaccurate and sometimes flagrantly false narratives to support the content of their delusional experiences. Patients with Capgras syndrome, for instance, believe that their loved ones have been replaced with imposters; individuals who suffer from this condition sometimes tell astonishingly complex stories regarding how this might have happened, and why; Korsakoff's syndrome frequently leads to memory loss which, in turn, makes people confabulate their past and construct fake memories; Anosognosia patients (Hirstein 2005) typically have an excuse up their sleeve for why they cannot move their (actually paralyzed) limbs; and so on. In all these cases, it is not people's working memory or their abstract thinking that is impaired. Nor are there are any dedicated cognitive modules going astray. Rather, people have lost (part of) their ability to critically reflect on whether what their consciousness manufactures is at all plausible – in light of what seems likely, what others tell them, or what coheres with what else they may know about the world. Impairments of Type II and Type III processing manifest in reduced cognitive ability or failures of cognitive monitoring and override of intuitive (and sometimes delusional beliefs) respectively. Think about it this way: we all know at least a little bit of what a delusional experience is like. A *déjà vu* episode contains the powerful experience that something – the thing that is currently happening – has already happened before. This impression can be very hard to shake, so much so that while we're in it, we (or, at least, I) sometimes try to figure out whether it didn't actually happen after all. But healthy people *override* this intuition and don't listen to it; instead, we simply wait it out and don't let this ephemeral delusion dictate any of the beliefs we would endorse upon reflection.

That there is a genuine difference between System II and III does not merely show up in characteristic forms of malfunctioning. Here is a second important reason for the triple process framework: Type II and

Type III processing can be teased apart by looking at which factors predict successful performance on various cognitive tasks known from the heuristics and biases literature. We have an extremely good understanding of what types of problems human cognitive systems have difficulties with, and social psychologists, behavioral economists and cognitive scientists have developed great expertise at coming up with cognitive traps suitable to expose those difficulties. But the fact is that not all cognitive errors are equal. Some are mainly correlated with cognitive ability, whereas some show little or no correlation with it; instead, performance on these tasks is predicted by people's *epistemic dispositions to engage in critical thinking*, that is, their propensity for Type III processing. For many cognitive tasks, marginal increases in intelligence don't help you very much. What is needed are a set of reflective thinking dispositions to engage in reasoning in the first place, and to let such reasoning have a genuine job to do that goes beyond mere rationalization of preexisting gut reactions.

I will argue that the majority of cases in which moral judgments, and in which normatively significant moral errors are made, are of the latter variety. Competent performance on these tasks depends on reflective level, Type III processing that allows people to second-guess their intuitions, consider different points of view, and enact a willingness to override one's intuition – even the most emotionally appealing ones – in favor of a more counterintuitive response.

Let me give a couple of examples. In a series of papers, Stanovich and West (2000 and 2008) have shown that many thinking biases are relatively independent of cognitive ability. The key thing to realize at this point is that from within the traditional System I/System II framework and the heuristics and biases literature, all cognitive errors are lumped together such that they all appear to be due to crude fast-and-frugal System I processing. The correct responses in these cognitive tasks would then be brought about by activation of System II. However, the mechanisms underwriting System II processing – the ability to engage in conscious, effortful reasoning, symbol-based thought, and fluid intelligence more generally – are not strongly predictive of optimal performance on many tasks. Something else must be going on.

Consider, for instance, the *belief-bias* effect. Here is a syllogism:

(1)   All living things need water.
(2)   Roses need water.
Therefore,   (3)   Roses are living things.

Now an argument counts as valid when its conclusion follows from it premises, that is, when the conclusion follows from the premises regardless of whether they are true. Validity is independent of the content of the propositions that form the premises. However, the majority, when given the above inference, think that the argument is valid, that is, that the premises logically entail the conclusion. But this is not so. It would be valid, for instance, to conclude from the fact that all living things need water and that roses are living things that roses need water. The false impression that the above syllogism is valid is driven by the truth of the above statements. All three statements are true – or at least highly believable – such that people are led to think that the inference is valid. Their belief in the conclusion and the premises biases their assessment of the logical validity of the inference.

Or, consider the famous ball/bat problem, which is a standard item in the so-called cognitive reflection task (CRT): a ball and a bat cost €1.10 together. The bat costs €1.00 more than the ball. How much does the ball cost? The obvious (but false) answer is 10 cents; the correct (but unobvious) answer is 5 cents. Correct performance on this test, too, isn't strongly predicted by cognitive ability.

Or, consider the so-called *Asian disease* case. Here, two groups of people are given a choice between two options regarding the onslaught of an unusual Asian disease. The first group can pick between policy programs A and B, which either save 200 people (from a group of 600) with certainty, or save 600 people with a 1/3 probability and save no one with a 2/3 probability, respectively. Programs C and D, which are given to the other group, will lead to the death of 400 people, or will have a 1/3 probability that no one dies and a 2/3 probability that 600 people die. The majority of the first group prefer program A to B, whereas the majority of the second prefer D to C, even though the choices (A/C and B/D) are identical.

Finally, an example with more recognizably moral content concerns *myside bias* (Stanovich and West 2007). Subjects from the US are more likely to agree that the sale of a German car should be banned in the US than they are that the sale of an American care should be banned in Germany even when the associated risks are the same.

In all of these cases, people make erroneous judgments not because of a lack of intelligence and processing power. Their mistakes are due to a failure to initiate and monitor conscious cognitive processing. It seems plausible enough that the ball costs 10 cents. Why think harder? Only people with a more benignly paranoid set of epistemic dispositions are motivated to think again, and eventually arrive at the correct response.

Thirdly, and arguably most importantly, the move from dual to triple process theory is motivated by the fact that dual process accounts do not supply what should be the core of *any* multi-process description of moral or non-moral cognition, which is a detailed and sufficiently rich account of how the stipulated processes – however many there are – interact. In particular, what is owed is how *intuition override* works. The main theoretical claim of the triple process theory here developed is that currently existing two systems accounts do not have many illuminating things to say about how the need for such override is detected, how it is initiated, monitored, and how its output is checked for accuracy.

This is despite the fact that, as I mentioned above, Social Intuitionism or Greene's Dual Process Account are essentially theories of intuitive override. But the problem is that these theories typically wave their hands at how this happens, and simply assume that, somehow, sometimes, it does happen. This is a striking fact in itself, particularly since these theories concede that our evolutionarily inherited and culturally shaped moral intuitions are unlikely to be a good fit for the modern social and natural conditions we find ourselves in (Greene 2014, 715).

What, in the end, is the core of Type II and III? In picking out the key feature of algorithmic Type II processing, Stanovich follows Leslie (1987) and, with some modifications, Nichols and Stich (2003) in arguing that System II is in charge of *cognitive decoupling*. System II's unique function is to take primary representations of the world – beliefs – "offline" and store them in a "Possible World Box" in which secondary representations can be manipulated without contaminating a subject's representation of the actual world. This allows processes of higher-order cognition to engage in hypothetical reasoning, move information around, test hypotheses, and so forth (see Figure 2.1).

Stanovich argues that the "raw ability to sustain such mental simulations while keeping the relevant representations decoupled is likely the key aspect of the brain's computational power" (50). The core feature of Type III, on the other hand, consists in the initiation, monitoring, and checking of such decoupling operations. Here, what matters most are epistemic dispositions to initiate critical, reflective-level thinking, which is then *carried out* by algorithmic cognition (see Figure 2.2).

The above considerations favor a tripartite structure of the mind in which the intuitive system ("TASS") is distinguished from an algorithmic

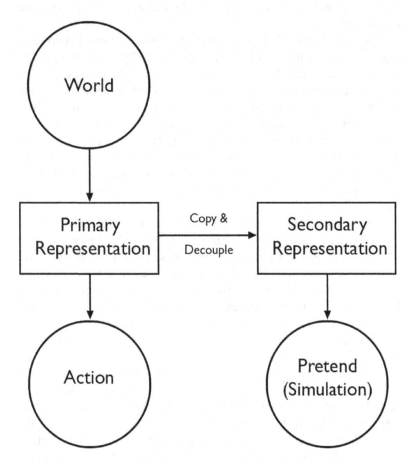

*Figure 2.1* Cognitive Decoupling (adapted from Stanovich 2011, 49)

level (aka System II) and a reflective level ("System III") which are in charge of carrying out and initiating, respectively, override of the default response generated by Type I processing.

## Moral bullshit

In 2016, Pennycook et al. (2015) were awarded the *Ig Nobel Peace Prize* for their research on bullshit, more precisely: people's receptivity to bullshit, especially when it is presented in pseudo profound disguise.[1] In particular, Pennycook and his colleagues were interested in the extent

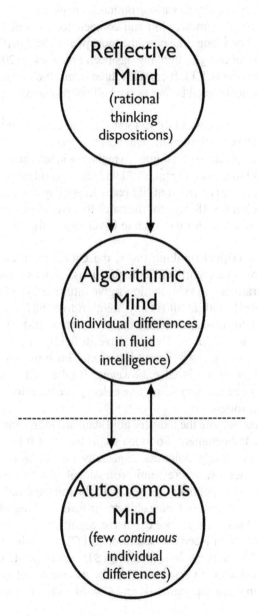

*Figure 2.2* The Tripartite Structure of the Mind (adapted from Stanovich 2009a, 58)

to which a subject's propensity to engage in critical reflective thinking affected their receptivity to various ominous deepities.

Assessing people's motivation and competence to think critically is no small feat. For a long time now, the most popular and perhaps easiest to use measure of analytic thinking has been Frederick's (2005) *Cognitive Reflection Task* (CRT). It contains three items, the first of which we have already encountered before as the ball/bat problem:

(1)  A bat and a ball cost $1.10 in total. The bat costs $1.00 more than the ball. How much does the ball cost? ___cents
(2)  If it takes 5 machines 5 minutes to make 5 widgets, how long would it take 100 machines to make 100 widgets? ___minutes
(3)  In a lake, there is a patch of lily pads. Every day, the patch doubles in size. If it takes 48 days for the patch to cover the entire lake, how long would it take for the patch to cover half of the lake? ___days

As with other critical thinking tasks, the CRT's main characteristic isn't that it poses inherently difficult questions, such as complex mathematical operations, that simply don't give intuitive Type I processing anything to work with at all (is any solution to 54687 x 11923 *intuitively* coming to mind?). Instead, the above three tasks are substantively fairly easy to solve. Their relative difficulty is due to the fact that they *deceptively cue* a default intuition. This intuition – 10 cents, 100 minutes, 24 days – is false, however.[2] It takes reflective thinking to detect the need for overriding those deceptive intuitions and to see the override through.

The CRT has become the industry gold standard for gauging individuals' epistemic temperament. So much so, in fact, that it is now starting to become increasingly pointless, especially for use in online survey tools such as *MTurk*, where semi-professional self-appointed guinea pigs have ceased to approach the test with the requisite naïveté (Haigh 2016). In order to assess their subjects' critical thinking ability, Pennycook et al. thus used a more extensive cognitive reflection task that includes measures of Need for Cognition (NFC), Actively Openminded Thinking (AOT), Superstitious Thinking (ST; here the score obtained by participants had to be reversed to reflect the inverse correlation between critical thinking and superstition)[3] and Consideration of Future Consequences (CfC).

Pennycook et al.'s study showed that there are great individual differences in bullshit receptivity. People with stronger reflective tendencies (and higher cognitive ability) are less likely to endorse pseudo profound bullshit statements such as "Attention and intention are the mechanics of manifestation" or "Matter is the experience in consciousness of a deeper non-material reality." Remarkably, people's bullshit receptivity score has great predictive power over a wide range of domains such as conspiracy theories, paranormal or religious belief, or alternative medicine – that is, everywhere where bullshit feels naturally at home.

The triple process account of moral cognition is mostly about reflecting on one's own intuitions, and overriding them when necessary. But it is at least equally important to be able to reflect upon and question *other people's* plausible-seeming statements. Pennycook and his colleagues have done a great job uncovering the epistemic dispositions that are necessary to pull this off. In fact, one could describe a person's poor critical thinking ability when it comes to questioning her own intuitions as a sort of high "internal" bullshit receptivity.

There is also moral bullshit. One way of characterizing the view developed in this book is to say that when it comes to morality, we are overly receptive to our own pseudo moral bullshit. This bullshit is delivered to us in the form of seemingly compelling, but often woefully inadequate intuitions. When these intuitions are *moral* intuitions, the consequences can be dire. We live in a modern world. This world is dynamic, complex, systemic, and anonymous, in short: the world we inhabit is counterintuitive. But our mind runs on intuitions. This is – or became – a questionable thing. Receptivity to pseudo moral bullshit used to be a harmless bug – or, indeed, no bug at all – because it worked for sorting out the moral infrastructure of closely knit tribal societies. But when powerful technologies and weird institutions are put into the hands of highly bullshit-receptive agents, things can get ugly.

## Moral reasoning

One of the most attention-grabbing findings in recent moral psychology concerns the phenomenon of moral dumbfounding (Haidt 2001 and 2012). Rationalists about moral judgment in particular tend to get a little nervous when the issue of dumbfounding is raised, because it seems to show that people's moral judgments are impervious to reason.

People are morally dumbfounded when they refuse to abandon their moral intuition in the absence of relevant reasons, or when the reasons the thought applied to the issue at hand have been debunked. Dumb-founding is most likely to occur in cases of taboo violations which are either harmless, or where it is unclear whether any harmful outcome is present ("offensive yet victimless"). Pertinent scenarios include the famous "Julie and Mark" vignette, in which two siblings on vacation decide to have consensual sex, eating one's dead pet dog, masturbating with a chicken carcass, or cleaning one's toilet with the (US) flag. Many subjects have a strong sense that these actions are wrong, but find it difficult to explain why. Importantly, they do not suspend their moral judgment once this becomes apparent because all the justifications they try to avail themselves of have been shown not to apply. Intuition carries the day; conscious reasoning has a hard time changing them. In short: moral dumbfounding is a kind of Type III intervention failure.

There is significant controversy regarding how best to interpret this finding. Haidt's preferred reading, obviously, is that the fact that people can be cornered into a state of dumbfounding shows that their moral judgments were never based on reasoning to begin with. It's intuitions all the way down, and conscious reasoning has at best a social function to perform.

However, there is the empirical issue that roughly 20% of subjects *did* revoke their initial judgment. Not so bad, one might think. Moreover, recent studies suggest that the problem with the dumbfounding vignettes is that people experience imaginative resistance upon reading them (Royzman, Kim and Leeman 2015; see also Guglielmo 2018). They simply do not buy that sex between siblings, even if consensual, won't do some sort of damage. That people "invent" harmful outcomes in cases of (allegedly) victimless transgressions is well established. Where there's a sin, there must be suffering: this is called "dyadic completion" (Gray, Schein and Ward 2014).

Perhaps more importantly, there simply *are* good reasons for disapproving of Julie and Mark's actions. Their decision is very morally risky, and the fact that – as the experimental devil's advocate insists – things turned out fine seems to have little or no bearing on the fact that they made a foolish decision (Jacobson 2012). People's moral intuition that there is something wrong with what the siblings did is likely due to a subtle appreciation of this point. Participants merely find it hard to articulate (Sauer 2017a).

So dumbfounding is tricky. Having said that, it would be implausible to deny that it exists, and is in fact widespread and pernicious.

Anecdotally, everyone knows tons of cases in which interlocutors (or oneself) stubbornly cling to their indefensible beliefs, unwilling to reconsider them. So what is going on here? A great feature of triple process moral psychology is that it offers a novel and convincing interpretation of the findings on dumbfounding. At its core, moral dumbfounding is a failure to initiate and/or carry out override of one's moral intuitions, especially when they are backed up by powerful emotions, which make the activation of critical moral thinking particularly difficult.

This seems to be a mere reinterpretation of the same finding, but it ends up making a significant difference when it comes to contextualizing the phenomenon of dumbfounding and the role of moral reasoning in moral judgment. It shows that dumbfounding does not support the anti-rationalist conclusions it is supposed to support. Rather, dumbfounding, being an instance of override failure, is to be expected. Cognitively penetrating one's emotionally charged gut reactions is difficult to do.

One of the main claims about moral reasoning made with the triple process account is this: moral reasoning can be carried out by System II alone, or by System II, initiated, monitored, and checked by System III. The former will frequently result in mere *post hoc* rationalization or outright confabulation, both of which are typically employed in the service of either moral obtuseness (= closed-mindedness) or – worse – moral disengagement (= the facilitation of morally objectionable conduct via reasoning, Hindriks 2015). Only Systems II *plus* III can therefore legitimately be described as being in the business of "default interventionism", because System II alone doesn't intervene at all.

The upshot is surprising: Haidt's original claim was that System II rarely changes people's moral intuitions. Rationalists were upset, and tried to come up with examples in which it does. But triple process theory says that Haidt was right all along: system II *is* wagged by the emotional dog. It *is* responsible for rationalization; only Type II *and* III that initiate genuine intuition override.

## Unleashing Type III

The core claim of triple process moral psychology is that competent moral judgment depends on intuitive override, and on the critical thinking dispositions that detect the need for, initiate, monitor, and check such override.

The result is a *default-interventionist* account of the structure of cognition. For what are essentially economic reasons, judgments about what to think, feel or do are largely made intuitively. It is only when those intuitions encounter an obstacle – something that isn't working, a mistake that has been pointed out to us – that the non-intuitive parts of the mind are engaged, and higher-order thinking is initiated. But how does this initiation happen?

According to the triple process account, the initiation of reflective intuition override is not, or at least not typically, executed by System II. Conscious reasoning in decoupling mode only occurs *after* the potential need for override and/or correction has been detected. This is the main job of "System" III, an individual's epistemic dispositions to engage in critical thinking in the first place.

It would be a mistake, however, to conclude that System I has either no role to play in this, or only the villain's. Remember the ball/bat problem again. Here, the problem is that the task cues an intuitively compelling but incorrect response. Now consider the following, slightly modified, task (Johnson, Tubau and de Neys 2016):

A magazine and a banana together cost $2.90.
The magazine costs $2.00.
How much does the banana cost?

Here, no one is even *tempted* to give an incorrect response. Why? A popular explanation for the average subject's poor performance in the ball/bat problem is that people think intuitively. When no intuition readily springs to mind because the question at hand is at least somewhat complicated, people simply substitute a simpler question and then answer *that one*. In the ball/bat problem, the substituted question could be how much the ball costs, given that the bat costs $1.00 and both cost $1.10, to which the median response – 10 cents – would indeed be the correct one. This substitution process is thought to occur at a subconscious level. Again, System I takes all the blame.

But this cannot be right. Johnson, Tubau and de Neys (2016) were able to show that already at the level of intuitive processing, people detect the potential need for intuitive override. When compared to a control task, such as the magazine/banana problem just mentioned, subjects who give the intuitive but incorrect response to the ball/bat problem are significantly less confident in their response and coming up with a judgment takes them more time. This suggests that their intuitions are always already sicklied o'er with the pale cast of thought. Importantly, putting participants under cognitive load, by making them simultaneously complete a memory task, does not diminish their "substitution sensitivity," which further confirms the hypothesis that this part of the critical thinking process sometimes takes place within System I.

The need for intuitive override is thus frequently detected at the level of intuitive processing. What it takes to get our critical thinking juices flowing is a healthy dose of epistemic queasiness, a "feeling of error" (Gangemi et al. 2015). The feeling of error is a critical thinking flag that sometimes comes attached to our intuitions.

This feeling of error, when present, has a decent degree of reliability. Gangemi and her colleagues found that when confronted with the usual suspects from the menu of critical thinking tasks, participants' feeling of error was not just much more pronounced compared to subjects dealing with non-deceptive control tasks. It was also significantly stronger, indicating a general propensity for detecting need for override.[4]

The feeling of error – and its close cousin, the general willingness to appreciate the *possibility* of error in one's intuitively formed beliefs – is the embodiment of a set of reflective epistemic dispositions. These are nicely summarized in a passage from Stanovich I quoted earlier, and comprise

> the tendency to collect information before making up one's mind, the tendency to seek various points of view before coming to a conclusion, the disposition to think extensively about a problem before responding, the tendency to calibrate the degree of strength of one's opinion to the degree of evidence available, the tendency to think about future consequences before taking action, the tendency to explicitly weigh pluses and minuses of situations before making a decision, and the tendency to seek nuance and avoid absolutism.
>
> (Stanovich 2011, 36)

One thing that stands in the way of unleashing Type III via the aforementioned critical thinking dispositions is confirmation bias (Nickerson 1998).[5] When assessing or justifying their beliefs, people have a tendency to seek out confirming rather than disconfirming evidence and are more likely to discount discordant information. Generally speaking, our minds seem to be on the defensive.

It should be noted that such "defensive" reasoning can play an important role, such as when it leads to efficiency gains in the epistemic division of labor of two or more people trying to make the best case for opposing points of view. It can also lead to beneficial downstream effects by shaping subsequent instances of moral judgment (Greenspan 2015). Today's rationalizations can become tomorrow's critical thinking aides.

In many cases, however, it does more harm than good. Intuitive override is always difficult to achieve, but the phenomenon of confirmation bias shows that our minds are literally rigged against it. Fortunately, there are kludges and work-arounds. The trick is to turn the defensive powers of cognition against itself.

How? One way of achieving this is through so-called *debunking arguments* (Sauer 2018). Debunking arguments do not attack the truth of a belief, but the justification one has for holding it. In many cases, they do so by supplying a genealogical explanation of how a subject came to hold a belief in an epistemically dubious or otherwise untrustworthy way. The key about such an explanation is that it has to demonstrate that, and how, the etiology of one's belief is *off track*, such that a subject would hold the (set of) belief(s) at issue whether they had been true or not.

Debunking arguments thus consist of at least two premises: a descriptive premise laying out the causal origins of a given belief and a normative premise revealing those origins to be unreliable or distortive. Together, they yield the debunking conclusion.

Why are debunking arguments so effective? One possible explanation for this is that when directly attacking the truth of a person's beliefs, the person immediately switches into defensive mode; guided – or seduced – by confirmation bias, one seeks to defend the truth of one's belief by coming up with buttressing evidence to corroborate it. This is a significant obstacle to critical thinking, because this process is designed to shield one's intuitions from the threat of revision. Override becomes the thing to be avoided at all epistemic cost.

Epistemic face-saving of this sort is as understandable as it is undesirable and unnecessary. Debunking arguments manage, to a certain extent at least, to bypass this problem. By providing only an indirect attack on a subject's beliefs, they disarm a subject's powers of epistemic self-defense and turn the reasoning process inward. Suppose that you have a bad feeling about someone else's behavior. It just seems wrong to you. Usually, you would take this impression at face value, and defend it when challenged, thus resisting the potential need to initi-ate a costly override of your intuition. But now suppose that instead of trying to *rebut* your moral intuition – for instance, by coming up with positive reasons for why the other person's behavior was not in fact wrong – I *undercut* it by pointing out to you that your judgment was formed in an unreliable way.[6] Perhaps I can show you video footage of how I primed you to respond negatively to a morally arbitrary feature of the situation? Or point out that your intuition is likely shaped by unconscious emotional reactions and biases? All of a sudden, defend-ing your belief in any straightforward way becomes at least somewhat awkward, because it doesn't engage with the problematic sources the belief originated in.

Some studies show that debunking arguments can be surprisingly effective. Remember that one of the core claims of the Social Intuition-ist model of moral judgment was that moral reasoning is more like a lawyer than a scientist. It is in the business of manufacturing rationali-zations for the emotionally charged intuitions one already holds, rather than following the argument where it leads. In a 2012 study, however, Paxton, Ungar, and Greene managed to show that under certain condi-tions, critical reflection can be effective in making subjects reconsider and/or abandon their initial moral gut reaction.

Let us return to the phenomenon of moral dumbfounding once more, which I described earlier as a typical instance of Type III/override failure. Subjects are reluctant to revoke their disapproval of consensual and pur-portedly harmless incest, even when challenged by an experimental devil's advocate. The main idea behind Paxton et al.'s study is that this reluc-tance varies depending – among other things, such as time to deliberate – on the *quality* of the argument subjects are dealing with.

To see how this works, consider the following two counterarguments two participants' anti-incest instance, which I will quote at length. First, there is a counterargument Paxton and his colleagues (correctly) describe as "weak":

> A brother – sister relationship is, by its [sic] nature, a loving relation-ship. And making love is the ultimate expression of love. Therefore, it makes perfect sense for a brother and sister, like Julie and Mark, to make love. If more brothers and sisters were to make love, there would be more love in the world, and that is a good thing. If broth-ers and sisters were not supposed to make love, then they wouldn't be sexually compatible, and yet they are. Brothers and sisters who

don't want to make love should at least try it once. There is nothing wrong with trying something once. Thus, it wasn't morally wrong for Julie and Mark to make love.

(170f.)

Their "strong" counterargument, on the other hand, reads like this:

For most of our evolutionary history, there were no effective con- traceptives, and so if siblings slept together they might conceive a child. Children born of such closely related parents would have a lower than normal likelihood of surviving. Thus, feelings of disgust toward incest probably evolved to prevent such children from being born. But in Julie and Mark's case, two kinds of contraception were used, so there was no chance of conceiving a child. The evolution- ary reason for the feeling of disgust is, therefore, not present in Julie and Mark's case. Any disgust that one feels in response to Julie and Mark's case cannot be sufficient justification for judging their behavior to be morally wrong.

(170)

No one who intuitively disapproved of Julie and Mark's actions will reconsider this intuition after reading the preposterously bad first argu- ment. In fact, considering the weak argument made subjects disapprove *more* strongly. The strong argument, however, had a marked effect on subjects' mean acceptability ratings and almost made them change their minds and straddle the midpoint on a 1–7 scale.

Notice, however, that the strong and weak arguments against peo- ple's anti-incest intuition do not just differ in quality, but in *type*. More precisely, the weak argument is a straightforward, albeit inadequate, attempt at a *rebuttal* of the intuition, whereas the strong argument aims to *undercut* the intuition with a debunking argument accusing the feel- ings of disgust which plausibly animate that intuition of being untrust- worthy. It is this feature, I suggest, that makes the strong argument so effective in making subjects reconsider their initial revulsion.

The effectiveness of turning the defensive powers of cognition against itself to facilitate critical thinking and intuitive override can also be demonstrated in another way. In particular, it is possible to harness the power of confirmation bias – and its flipside, which is the motivation to disconfirm opposing points of view – for the greater epistemic good. In a fascinating study, Trouche et al. combined the insight that people evaluate others' beliefs and supporting arguments more critically with a choice blindness design (Johansson et al. 2005). In the first phase, participants were given five elliptical syllogisms to evaluate by indicating, through multiple choice, which statement followed from the information they were initially given. They were also given the opportunity to provide a short explanation for their answer. In the second phase, subjects were allowed to take another look at their answers, along with the answers given by a previous participant and her explanation. In one of five cases, however, the solution and explanation they had given *themselves* were presented to them as if it were someone else's answer. Their own alleged answer was altered to match this change. Actually, they received the objectively valid answer (if they had answered invalidly) or the most common invalid answer (if they had picked the valid option). Around half of the participants detected this change. In the manipulated condition, subjects rejected what were in fact their own answers in 56% of cases. Crucially, evaluating their own arguments as ones purportedly produced by someone else *improved* their reasoning ability. Critical thinking ability is increased when subjects are artificially forced to be epistemically impartial.

## Scaffolding critical thinking

The most obvious policy lever there is for improving Type III processing may seem to be to instill reflective dispositions to engage in critical thinking directly. It may seem worthwhile, for instance, to provide people with the opportunity to develop and cultivate desirable cognitive traits. To illustrate with an example, consider *intellectual humility*. Alfano et al. (2017) suggest that intellectual humility comprises various dimensions, perhaps the most important of which are open-mindedness, intellectual modesty, engagement, and corrigibility.[7] It fosters the exercise of critical thinking to acknowledge the limitations of one's knowledge; to not obsess over how one's cognitive prowess is being perceived by others; to be prepared to improve one's understanding of issues; and not to panic in response to encountering that one may have been wrong about something.

As with all virtuous traits, there are complementary vices. Open-mindedness is opposed to epistemic arrogance; modesty to vanity; engagement to a lack of curiosity; and corrigibility to a fragile sense of intellectual self-worth. Interestingly, Alfano and colleagues also include less intuitively obvious epistemic dispositions in their list of features of intellectual humility. Intellectual Macchiavellianism, for instance, is the tendency to manipulatively extract information from others; intellectual kleptomania makes people pass off others' ideas as their own. Both of these features are interesting not just because they undermine an individual's own critical thinking ability. They also have a tendency to undermine the very rules of knowledge generation as a mutually cooperative enterprise.

I am using intellectual humility only as one possible example. When it comes to improving critical thinking dispositions and intuitive override, targeting cognitive virtues is always at least a viable option. But a healthy dose of skepticism remains in order: as Alfano himself has noted, epistemic situationism suggests that people's epistemic character may be just as fragile as their character more generally (Doris 2002). People's epistemic dispositions are situationally indexed, and do not always manifest cross-situationally.[8]

One possible solution for this situational variability could be to provide external support for subjects' frail cognitive dispositions. In recent years, it has become increasingly fashionable to reject the idea that the mind is confined to the boundaries of the skull (Clark and Chalmers 1998, Clark 2008, Menary 2010). Instead, many authors now defend the claim that features of the environment – such as technical artifacts or environmental cues – can be considered a proper part of people's minds. The examples range from smartphones or notebooks to regular conversation partners and social institutions. How conceptually plausible and empirically convincing strong versions of this extension thesis are is not important for my purposes here (Sterelny 2010). What matters is that to function well, and often even to function at all, our minds require all kinds of external support.

A useful metaphor for this is environmental *scaffolding*. Humans have an excellent ability to offload (components of) tasks onto their immediate or remote environment. And they may be virtually unique in outsourcing and recruiting external support for cognitive tasks. We use alarm-clocks, pencil and paper, cookbooks, measurement devices, and spouses to navigate the natural and social world. Frequently, this comes not just with increases in precision and accuracy, but with enormous gains in efficiency. Relying on external cognitive aides frees up internal cognitive resources. In fact, almost everything we do depends on such scaffolding. Without it, we wouldn't be able to do much at all.

The extended mind hypothesis and the concept of external scaffolding can be just as fruitfully applied to agency and decision-making.

The extended mind does not merely support traditional cognitive operations such as memory, mental arithmetic, or spatial cognition. Most of the more interesting things we do require non-trivial amounts of foresight, resilience, willpower, and self-control. These executive capacities admit of, and indeed require, external scaffolding, too. The extended will is supported by various volitional prostheses that function as constraints, nudges or commitment devices and allow people to realize their goals in the face of countervailing temptations and distractions (Heath and Anderson 2010).

The powers of scaffolding can be recruited to create environments which are either conducive to critical thinking or detrimental to it. This is especially true in modern societies. These societies have come with enormous accomplishments. Three of Abraham Lincoln's four children died before reaching adulthood. But modern gains in health and welfare in developed countries have caused infant mortality to plummet, and most other indicators of wellbeing and affluence to rise. At the same time, the institutions that made these gains possible in the first place constitute a deeply hostile mental environment. Virtually all of the most important social functions in modern societies are performed by institutions which are offensive to our default mode of thinking. Neither how the allocation of resources (markets), nor how collective decision-making (democratic politics), the development and enforcement of rules (law), the generation of knowledge (science), or the procedural and informational background holding them all together (bureaucracy) are organized make sense on a visceral level.

In addition to the general counterintuitiveness of modern institutions, many of the most distinctive aspects of modern living are positively toxic for the initiation and proper execution of critical reflective thinking. Heath's (2014a) call for "slow politics" is as justified as it is naïve (as he himself acknowledges), the idea being that if only one could introduce structural changes to political discourse and the media that would allow certified experts to explain the concept of comparative advantage, the ripple effects of global warming, the risk-pooling advantages of single-payer health care or the deadweight losses imposed by immigration restrictions to an audience prepared to listen carefully to a nationally broadcast mini lecture, everything would be fine. Instead, the contemporary media landscape feeds the masses superficially compelling nonsense and casts critical thinking – open-mindedness, need for understanding and cognition, resistance to myside bias, skepticism towards simple but intuitively plausible beliefs – in a morally dubious light.

This is a huge problem because, as I quoted earlier,

> the decontextualizing demands of modernity increasingly require such characteristics as: fairness, rule-following despite context, even-handedness, nepotism prohibitions, unbiasedness, universalism, inclusiveness, contractually mandated equal treatment, and discouragement of familial, racial, and religious discrimination. These requirements are difficult ones probably for the reason that they override processing defaults related to the self.
>
> (Stanovich 2011, 76)

Modern societies are thus inherently rigged against the successful intervention of Type III processing and intuitive override. Now it would of course be highly commendable to scaffold our critical thinking capacities to bolster the quality of our cognitive output. But that doesn't mean that it is likely to happen anytime soon, especially given that this lamentable situation is self-reinforcing.

## Notes

1 That same year, the Ig Nobel Prize for Chemistry went to *Volkswagen* for "solving the problem of excessive automobile pollution emissions by automatically, electromechanically producing fewer emissions whenever the cars are being tested."
2 The correct answers are, again, 5, 5, and 47.
3 See Toplak, West, & Stanovich (2014). Moreover, they supplemented the CRT, in collaboration with its original creator, with the following items:

(4)   If John can drink one barrel of water in 6 days, and Mary can drink one barrel of water in 12 days, how long would it take them to drink one barrel of water together? _____ days [correct answer = 4 days; intuitive answer = 9]

(5)   Jerry received both the 15th highest and the 15th lowest mark in the class. How many students are in the class? _____ students [correct answer = 29 students; intuitive answer = 30]

(6)   A man buys a pig for $60, sells it for $70, buys it back for $80, and sells it finally for $90. How much has he made? _____ dollars [correct answer = $20; intuitive answer = $10]

(7)   Simon decided to invest $8,000 in the stock market one day early in 2008. Six months after he invested, on July 17, the stocks he had purchased were down 50%. Fortunately for Simon, from July 17 to October 17, the stocks he had purchased went up 75%. At this point, Simon has: a. broken even in the stock market, b. is ahead of where he began, c. has lost money [correct answer = c, because the value at this point is $7,000; intuitive response = b].

4 For a general account of metacognition, see Proust 2013.
5 for an intriguing attempt at "rehabilitating" confirmation bias, see Mercier and Sperber 2011.

6 On the distinction between rebutting and undercutting defeaters, see Pollock 1987.
7 The point here is not to supply a watertight definition of the concept of intellectual humility, but to come up with a workable operationalization that allows the identification and measurement of this trait in an empirical context.
8 It is important to note that my triple process account claims that, as a matter of empirical fact, there are individual differences between people with respect to their epistemic dispositions – that is, certain intellectual character traits. Some are more willing to question their own intuitions, others less. This puts my account in tension with epistemic situationism (Alfano 2011).

# 3 A triple process theory of moral cognition

## Triple process moral psychology: an outline

Triple Process Moral Psychology is a comprehensive account of moral judgment and reasoning. The main idea behind it is that moral judgment is only insufficiently understood when described in terms of an automatic System I and a conscious System II. Moral judgment is based on an integrated network of intuitive, algorithmic, and reflective processing. Sometimes, these three elements conflict. Sometimes, they cooperate.

Like most other theories of moral cognition, the Triple Process framework proposed here acknowledges the essentially intuitive basis of moral judgment. At the same time, it suggests that the key to *competent* moral judgment is how subjects manage and, if necessary, override their intuitions. Such intuition override, the conditions under which it happens, the circumstances under which it fails to happen, and the psychological resources necessary to make it happen form the core of the theory.

All of this leads to a richer account of the structure of cognition (see Figure 3.1). There are sound empirical and conceptual reasons for why intuitive override cannot be executed solely by the kind of conscious processing typically described as System II. System II needs to be complemented by a further type of processing which is in charge of detecting the need for initiating override, monitoring its execution, and checking its results for accuracy. This *third* type of processing consists of a set of epistemic dispositions to engage in conscious reasoning in the first place, and a variety of knowledge structures that enable such reasoning to be successful. Together, these *reflective* dispositions and the *mindware* that makes them efficacious constitute System III. The third type of processing is responsible for the critical evaluation of our moral intuitions. It also accounts for when and why this critical evaluation doesn't occur, and how this leads to moral error.

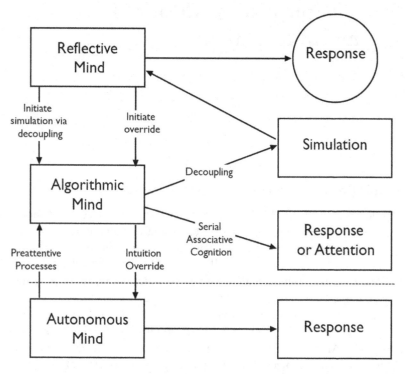

*Figure 3.1* The structure of cognition: initiation, decoupling, and override (adapted from Stanovich 2011, 62)

Many people will suspect that the difference between Dual and Triple process theory is merely semantic. But I think that this suspicion is unwarranted. There are sound empirical, conceptual, and normative reasons for moving towards a triple process account of moral cognition. The third type is *real*. And if you enjoyed moving from a dual to a triple process framework, you have something to look forward to in the next decade or so, because there may indeed be *four* types of processing.[1] Triple process theory is based on the idea that System II needs to be further internally distinguished into a reflective and an algorithmic type of processing. But it is not just System II that can be partitioned into Type II and III. System I allows for further differentiation as well.

We have already seen that automatic Type I cognition comprises a variety of modular types of processing from catching a ball to recognizing faces, reading, and so forth. Some of these functions may be hard-wired and some overlearned. In addition to this, Evans (2009) suggests that there is a more general, systematic distinction to be made within

System I, namely one between *autonomous* and *preattentive* Type I processes. This means that there are *two* dual process distinctions – one between preattentive and analytic, and the other between autonomous and analytic processes. Autonomous processes "control behavior directly without need for any kind of controlled attention" (42). Preattentive processes, on the other hand, first need to "supply content into working memory" (42) to become operative (see Figure 3.2).

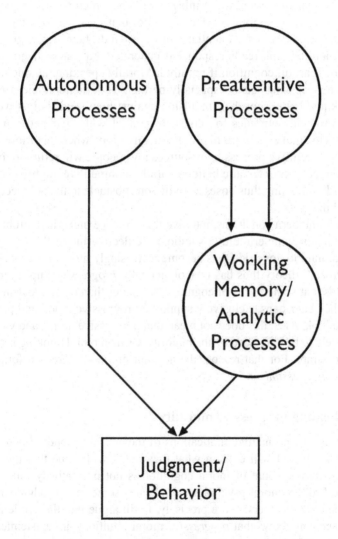

*Figure 3.2* System I: Autonomous and Preattentive Processing (adapted and modified from Evans 2009, 43)

The interaction of Type I and Type II can thus be parallel-competitive (both Type I and Type II/III generate a judgmental or behavioral response, only one of which can "win") or default-interventionist: in this latter case, Type I processing suggests a default response, which often receives at least minimal (and frequently biased) scrutiny by higher-order thinking, and can be intervened upon when deemed necessary. Examples for parallel processing, on the other hand, are a gambler's awareness of the gambler's fallacy, which persists in parallel with their behaviorally effective belief that they will win the next round. Examples for sequential conflict include heuristic cognition, where a rough-and-ready response is generated, but can be overridden by more careful cognition if required. Morally speaking, autonomous Type I processing seems especially pernicious: a homophobic person may know better, but their revulsion against homosexuals just won't go away, and continues to persist in parallel with their better judgment. This makes it more likely that in situations where emotions run high, or cognitive processing resources low, people will return to these epistemically problematic beliefs. Parallel-competitive, highly encapsulated processing thus poses a continuous obstacle to the prospects of moral progress.

Under modern conditions, intuitive thinkers face unintuitive problems that call for counterintuitive solutions. Reflective moral thinking and critical intuition override thus become increasingly more important. Triple Process theory thus has unapologetically *progressive* implications. It holds that some forms of cognition are better than others, and shows that the better ones exclusively support a progressive moral and political outlook. Alas, this does not mean that progressive norms and values are likely to be embraced by the majority. Critical moral thinking is real, but it is rare. For that reason, the account proposed here is a form of *rationalist pessimism*.

## Vindicating progressive morality

What are the normative implications of the account proposed here? In this third part, I will explain what they are. I will argue that the Triple Process Account of moral cognition is not normatively innocent. Triple Process moral psychology vindicates some moral judgments at the expense of others. More precisely, I will argue that the Triple Process account shows that *progressive* moral intuitions are epistemically and morally preferable to conservative moral intuitions. Triple process moral psychology suggests not only that there can be moral change, but that it has a *direction*.

In the most general terms, the Triple Process case for progressive moral judgments can be expressed like this: our mind runs on intuitions. But many of these intuitions, and the processes that generate them, are subject to various well-understood but nevertheless recalcitrant bugs which make it frequently problematic to rely on them for moral guidance. The moral intuitions resulting from these bugs need to be overridden. Individual critical thinking dispositions and crystallized moral mindware (more on which below) make such override possible. Those moral beliefs which are the upshot of cognitive processes that filter our moral intuitions through such mindware-enhanced reflective dispositions are *comparatively* more likely to be justified than those who are not.

In making this suggestion, I am not deriving an "ought" from an "is" – whatever this means. Rather, I will assume that the cognitive processes sketched here, at least under the conditions that matter, are epistemically superior to the uninhibited autonomous mind. Those who reject this assumption to begin with are therefore unlikely to be convinced by the normative arguments that follow.

I will assume that some form of moral constraint is needed to secure mutually beneficial forms of cooperation. Under modern conditions, this form can only be a framework of morality that relies, to a very large extent, on overriding our more primitive moral instincts. The resulting moral beliefs will therefore be ones which are supported and facilitated by critical moral reasoning. And critical moral reasoning is best understood as an interaction of Type II and Type III resources which monitor and override our Type I moral intuitions when necessary. This is a *vindicating* argument for the moral judgments that result from reflective Type III cognition.[2]

The problem is that modern forms of cooperation and the institutions that maintain them are deeply un- and even counterintuitive. They are only accessible to cognitive outputs that have survived at least some reflective scrutiny. This is not, in principle, a new problem. The persistence

of evolution-shaped behaviours in radically altered cultural settings is at the core of human historical development. Consciousness of the fact that the original conditions no longer apply often has little effect on patterns of behaviour determined by deeply engrained, evolution-shaped, proximate stimuli.

(Gat 2008, 130)

Other evolutionary theorists have made similar points:

> If we are correct, the institutions that foster hierarchy, strong leadership, inegalitarian social relations, and an extensive division of labor in modern societies are built on top of a social "grammar" originally adapted to life in tribal societies. To function, humans construct a social world that resembles the one in which our social instincts evolved. At the same time, a large-scale society cannot function unless people are able to behave in ways that are quite different from what they would be in small-scale tribal societies. Labor must be finely divided. Discipline is important, and leaders must have formal power to command obedience. Large societies require routine, peaceful interactions between unrelated strangers. These requirements necessarily conflict with ancient and tribal social instincts, and thus generate emotional conflict, social disruption, and inefficiency.
>
> (Richerson and Boyd 2005, 230)[3]

If – and *only* if – we want to reap the benefits which modern, counter-intuitive forms of social organization make possible, then we must rely on the authority of critical moral thinking, and suppress our tribal moral intuitions.

What are the normative implications Stanovich himself derives from his model? He suggests that a gene-centered account of evolution entails that an organism's evaluative dispositions are in no way guaranteed to promote the interests *of the organism*. Rather, individual organisms are (metaphorically speaking) the machines genes have built to create copies of themselves. In the case of human beings, genes have found a way to equip their protective vessels with domain-general reasoning mechanisms that will make them able to flexibly respond to a changing environment. Little did they know that these very capacities would eventually allow their humans to become aware of the fact that their own interests and the interests of their genes can come apart. This leads to a "robot's rebellion" (Stanovich 2005) during which human thinkers can reflectively decide to *disregard* their genes' interests. We can use contraception to get the pleasure of sex without furthering our genes' interest in procreation. This dynamic, however, is difficult to put to rest. Once we start rejecting the authority of our evolutionary heritage, it becomes unclear which interests remain. Why have children? Why avoid pain? Why, indeed, stay alive at all?

Although I am sympathetic to Stanovich's recommendation to "put the vehicle first" (2005, 78ff.), I will adopt a slightly different approach. How, again, can we use the Triple Process account to distinguish between correct and incorrect moral judgments? Stanovich (2009a, 56) notes that the most cognitively able subjects give the instrumentally rational response in many heuristics and biases tasks, where the modal (i.e. most frequent) response is the erroneous, but evolutionarily adaptive one. Now this observation, I wish to suggest, can be used to construct something akin to a reverse inference in neuroscience (Poldrack 2006; cf. Machery 2014): cognitively able subjects choose response R in non-moral task T; response R is the correct one; cognitively able subjects also choose response R* in moral task M; therefore, response R* is likely the correct one, too. This is a type of vindicating argument, which assumes that people who tend to be right about a variety of non-moral thinking tasks also tend to be right about moral thinking tasks. This inference is certainly not watertight, but until there is an explanation for why an individual's superior cognitive abilities should have a *detrimental* effect on their moral judgment, or at least no effect at all, the onus is on those who reject it to explain what grounds the asymmetry.

I have said that the Triple Process account has *progressive* moral implications. What do I mean by this? Here, I wish to follow Michael Huemer's account of a "liberal" moral outlook, about which he writes:

> When I speak of liberalism, I intend, not any precise ethical theory, but rather a certain very broad ethical orientation: liberalism (1) recognizes the moral equality of persons, (2) promotes respect for the dignity of the individual, and (3) opposes gratuitous coercion and violence. So understood, nearly every ethicist today is a liberal. But while this broad orientation is mostly uncontroversial today, this does not render the category of liberalism uninteresting, for as we shall see, human history has been dominated by highly illiberal views.
>
> The three aspects of liberalism named above are not simply three unrelated moral commitments. Liberalism is a coherent ethical perspective. The idea that individuals should be treated with dignity fits

together with the idea that individuals are moral equals, and that one should eschew violence and coercion against the individual. [. . .] This is not to deny that there might be other reasonable candidates for correct ethical orientations; it is only to say that liberalism ought to be counted high on the list of initially plausible candidates

(Huemer 2016, 1987)

Progressivism is a cluster of mutually supportive views that focuses on the reduction of gratuitous harm, the improvement of people's lives along the major dimensions of health and wealth, the reduction of arbitrary privileges and discrimination, and a commitment to the basic equality of all sentient beings. Importantly, it promotes the *reshaping* of local and global institutions to serve those goals. As such, it is committed to *change for the better*, whenever such change is feasible.

It should be noted that the range of possible moralities that qualify as progressive can, on my view, be extremely broad. Progressiveness in one's moral outlook is compatible with quite radical disagreements on policy. Progressive moral views encompass anything from hard-core libertarians to radical egalitarian leftists. My argument, then, is supposed to show that whatever the correct moral-political outlook is, it is likely to be a progressive, rather than a conservative, one. But since many, if not most, progressive moral frameworks are mutually incompatible, they cannot all be true at the same time. This means that the converse conclusion is unjustified: I am not suggesting that because a moral view is progressive, it is therefore likely to be correct, only that if it is correct, then it is likely to be progressive.

Note, also, that my argument relies on the assumption that we do, in fact, live in modern societies with distinctively modern institutions and cognitive demands. It is not in and of itself an argument that such social arrangements would be preferable even if we didn't already inhabit them – although I happen to think that such an argument could be made.[4] Rather, it builds the case for non-intuitive (and indeed counterintuitive) moral thinking on the fact that we have inherited a set of moral intuitions which are tailor-made for specific social structures and that these moral intuitions have not only outlived their usefulness, but frequently become positively harmful.[5] In certain contexts, sticking to evolved moral intuitions makes everyone worse off.[6] This is what makes intuitive override so important.

My main aim is to develop a vindicating argument for progressive moral and political attitudes. But I also have a more modest aim, which is to determine what the normative implications of this account could be if it were correct. What I am trying to do in this book is to take an existing, empirically well-supported framework in cognitive science, and apply it to the issue of moral cognition. This is a legitimate endeavor in its own right. It then becomes an interesting question what the normative implications of this framework could be. After taking a second look at the evidence, so to speak, it becomes clear that the processes of reflective intuitive override which are plausibly implicated in producing moral judgments are strongly associated with a particular type of normative belief. The normative implications of Triple Process moral psychology, if there are any, are what this evidence suggests.

Finally, I would like to stress that for the purposes of this book, I treat people's moral and political beliefs as belonging to the same category. It is clear that people's moral beliefs heavily influence their political attitudes. In addition to this, many of the most interesting cases of personal normative beliefs simply cannot be meaningfully assigned to only one of the two categories: people's attitudes towards immigration, fairness, sexuality, or the economy and the policy beliefs they hold about these issues form one cohesive cluster of moral-political beliefs. These beliefs concern what people ought to do, and how society should be run.

My view differs from earlier attempts to derive normative conclusions from intuitive override on the basis of the descriptive premises of multi-process moral psychology. The received view is Greene's dual process theory, whose outlines I have already summarized above. Perhaps the most popular claim made by the dual process account of moral cognition is that intuitive override is characteristically connected to consequentialist moral judgment. People need more time to arrive at the consequentialist verdict in moral-personal dilemmas because even though they feel the pull of the deontological prohibition, some choose to override it in favor of saving the greater number.

It is unfortunate that Greene labeled the two subtypes of moral judgment he wishes to debunk and vindicate, respectively, "deontological" and "consequentialist." It seems that *absolutist* and *flexible* would have been vastly preferable labels, not only because this would have spared him a lot of Kantian vitriol, but also because this distinction would have captured the essence of the opposition he has in mind – rigid prohibitions and context-sensitive cost/benefit analysis, respectively – far better than the "traditional" labels borrowed from the textbooks.

I wish to show, contra Greene, that replacing the simple dual process account with triple process moral psychology shows that progressive moral intuitions are epistemically superior to conservative moral beliefs. In more recent work, Greene himself has moved on from his orthodox utilitarian position. The position he now advocates is labeled *deep pragmatism* (Greene 2013), and the normative commitments this position embodies are perhaps best described as facilitating cooperative endeavors for the sake of increasing general welfare. *Modulo* this change, there is much in Greene's argument I agree with.

There is a lot of evidence that some sort of multi-process model of moral judgment is correct (Greene 2014). Greene holds that controlled cognition preferentially supports consequentialist moral judgments. I wish to argue that critical thinking supports moral judgments resulting from intuition override, which can be deontological *or* consequentialist. Below, I will suggest that a good umbrella term for such counterintuitive judgments is "progressive." This, I will also suggest, partially vindicates those judgments. Moreover, the evidence Greene points to shows that interfering with executive control, and other higher-level control states (i.e. Type III), rather than just interfering with serial processing ability or working memory (i.e. Type II), has an important impact on moral judgment.

For one thing, there is evidence that moral judgment often involves conflict resolution between competing considerations. It is misleading to suggest that deontological reasoners are blind to utilitarian considerations. They are usually sensitive to both, and merely resolve that tension in favor of the latter. It is thus fair to say that sometimes, intuitive override ends up siding with the deontological option. There is no *a priori* connection between override and consequentialism (Białek and de Neys 2016).

Kahane et al. (2012; cf. Paxton, Bruni and Greene 2013) have shown that that there are both counterintuitive deontological and consequentialist judgments. The reason why Greene's work winds up suggesting that consequentialism is uniquely associated with intuition override is that in the stimuli he used, the consequentialist option always happened to be the counterintuitive one. If Kahane is right, then the reason why in Greene's studies consequentialist judgments took more time is not that they are specifically associated with override of deontological intuitions (though they sometimes are). The reason is that the consequentialist options were selected to be counterintuitive; when deontological judgments are the counterintuitive ones, *they* are the ones it takes longer to arrive at. There is thus simply no connection between engaging in override and a particular normative option. There is, however, a connection between override and counterintuitive judgments. And since counterintuitive moral beliefs tend to be progressive, the vindicating argument Greene had in mind for consequentialism gets redirected to progressivism. That is my argument here.

The elective affinity between types of cognitive processing and where moral/political beliefs fall on the progressive/conservative spectrum enjoys strong empirical support.[7] Both the association between reflective thinking and progressive attitudes on the one hand as well as the link between miserly processing and conservatism on the other are well explored. Let me start with the latter.

Consider, first, how autonomous processing is implicated in conservative attitudes. Conservatism emphasizes personal responsibility, endorses relations of hierarchy, and is partial towards the status quo. Eidelman et al. (2012; see also van Berkel et al. 2015), who demonstrate a relation between critical thinking and egalitarian values) conducted four studies to test the relative contribution of different types of cognitive processing to people's political beliefs. Their second and third study are only indirectly relevant for my purposes because they manipulated Type II processing – rather than the reflective Type III that I am primarily interested in here[8] – either by putting participants under cognitive load or by inducing time pressure. Their first and fourth study, however, more directly manipulate Type III processing by looking at the effects of alcohol intoxication ("Study 1 was conducted in vivo at a local bar," 809) on people's "epistemic motivation" (814) as well as encouragement of effortful thinking:

> [P]articipants were told to "think hard about each term before responding. Don't give your first response. Instead, really put forth effort and consider the issue. Take your time and give a careful and thoughtful response." In the *low-effort processing* condition, participants were told to "give your first, immediate response to the terms. Don't think too hard about your response; don't debate yourself. Instead, go quickly and give your first, initial response to the terms as soon as you read them."
>
> (814)

In both cases, it was found that uncritical processing promotes conservative attitudes. The case of inebriation is of particular interest here because alcohol selectively impairs self-monitoring, inhibition, self-control, and executive functioning, in short: intuition override (Heath and Hardy-Vallée 2015). This provides direct support for the negative correlation between critical thinking and non-progressive attitudes.

At least as important, and perhaps more well-known, are studies confirming the link between conservative attitudes and various affective reactions. Notoriously, conservatives score high on disgust sensitivity (Inbar, Pizarro and Bloom 2009). But they also score higher on propensity to fear. Indeed, perceiving the fabric of society as well as law and order as threatened by change or disruption could be seen as *the* hallmark of conservatism. Accordingly, conservatism as a moral-political orientation is strongly predicted by factors such as death anxiety and fear of loss and threat; negative correlations can be observed with regard to uncertainty tolerance, openness to new experiences, and dogmatism/ambiguity intolerance (Jost et al. 2003). This increase in susceptibility to fear has interesting epistemic ramifications. Fessler, Pisor and Holbrook (2017) found that conservatives are more likely to believe – that is, assign higher credibility to – statements with threatening content (such as "Hotel room keycards are often encoded with personal information that can be read by thieves" or "Terrorist attacks in the U.S. have increased since Sept 11, 2001"). Conversely, one can make progressives think more like conservatives by making them feel threatened (Nail et al. 2009).

The evidence for a link between Type III thinking and progressive moral/political attitudes is at least as unambiguous. This pattern is on display not just when comparing WEIRD to non-WEIRD cultures (Henrich et al. 2010), but also within one and the same cultural context (Talhelm et al. 2015).[9] Liberal attitudes can also be promoted directly by priming analytical thinking. People's propensity to engage in critical thinking supports more progressive, that is: liberal, egalitarian, individualistic, welfare-oriented moral judgments.[10] I will return to this issue below.

When it comes to progressive moral attitudes, the role of external scaffolding starts to play an important role again. For instance, the classic "contact hypothesis" is that being around lots of other people with different lifestyles, preferences or races will make people more accepting of diversity. This serves as an example for how social scaffolding can improve critical thinking: presumably, an aversion to other people on the basis of race, sexual orientation or lifestyle is typically unjustified, and promotes harmful ingroup/outgroup tribalism. It can even have disastrous economic effects through protectionist thinking. A diverse environment, for instance a large, non-segregated city, will typically scaffold people's ability to discount or compensate for certain recalcitrant biases against "outgroup" members:

> The evidence for this learning is not merely anecdotal. In the United States national surveys and surveys in the South have shown the

greater contact with gay persons goes with increased tolerance toward gay sex and gay marriage [. . .]. The change in moral judgments is consistent with social contact theory [. . .], where social contact can itself be seen as a form of moral learning in this case. In effect, social contact breaks the gayness-bad-character link and also the larger association of gayness with unnaturalness, depravity, and lack of humanity. Once these links are broken, moral foundations tend to line up in favor of permitting gay sex and gay marriage. At least this kind of learning process leading to a major change in moral perspective is psychologically possible in light of the basic social and psychological mechanisms of moral learning.

(Campbell 2017)

To a certain extent, the epistemic dispositions to seek out new information, consider alternative points of view, and stay open-minded can be institutionalized in people's external environment.

A further reason why moral learning should be expected to consist in a move towards more progressive moral outlooks is this: as I have argued elsewhere (Sauer 2017a) moral judgment is based on educated and rationally amenable moral intuitions. These intuitions are shaped, to a large extent, via feedback loops that emerge from moral reasoning as a social practice of giving and asking for reasons. This social practice has a *challenge-and-response* structure: moral intuitions are not deduced from first principles (Koralus and Alfano 2017). They are taken from a reservoir or culturally transmitted beliefs which are taken for granted (hinge propositions, as it were). As social complexity increases through functional differentiation and division of labor and simple increases to scale, the game of giving and asking for reasons – i.e. *language* – starts playing a bigger and bigger role in cultural reproduction and securing social integration. Consequently, the internal logic of reason-giving practices ends up "biasing" social developments in its own direction of greater universality, symmetry, and equality. As a result, our moral intuitions start becoming more "progressive," because they are structured to an ever greater extent by the particularly modern shape the game of giving and asking for reasons has taken. That way, critical thinking dispositions (Type III processing) become externally embodied in the linguistic practices of cultural reproduction characteristic for modern societies (Heath 2014b).

The link between epistemic improvements and progressive attitudes also shows up in public opinion research (Caplan 2007, 25ff.; see also Althaus 2003). People's so-called "enlightened preferences" – which are statistically simulated by surveying their policy preferences, political knowledge, demographic information, and then gauging what they would endorse if they were equipped with improved political knowledge – are unequivocally more progressive. The better informed are less interventionist and less supportive of war, but more pro-choice, supportive of gay rights, and more skeptical of religion. They are more in favor of free trade, equality of opportunity, and immigration. These changes show a clear pattern.

But Triple Process theory does not shed light only on the moral – what is right or wrong, what we owe to each other, or what the appropriate objects of guilt and resentment are. It also has something to say about the *ethical*, that is, questions of what constitutes a good and meaningful life, and which traits should be cultivated or suppressed, respectively, in order to have one. Remember that Triple Process theory holds that many conflicts between the modal and the correct response in cognitive tasks reflects a distinction between promoting what's adaptive on the subpersonal level and what's optimal on the personal level. The modal response is typically the one that would have been adaptive for our genes in our environment of evolutionary adaptedness; the "expert" response is typically the one that is best for the whole organism/person – that is, the smallest unit at which ascriptions of rationality and irrationality start making sense. Now what about *ethical*, rather than more narrowly moral, judgments? Here, we can say that various undesirable traits – vices, really – such as jealousy, envy, revenge, cowardice, and subservience – frequently reflect dispositions which serve our genes' (metaphorical) interests, rather than our own. Jealousy or envy and other ethical vices are much more *harmful to ourselves* than we intuitively think. What about happiness and the good life? That there is a link between progressive attitudes and happiness is widely doubted (Schlenker, Chambers and Le 2012). People generally claim that conservatives are happier. However, this seems to be due to self-reports, rather than actual happiness. Wojcik et al. (2015) show that conservatives report, but liberals display, greater happiness. Triple Process Theory is good for you!

## Initiating override: reflective dispositions and Type III failure

If one had to pick the main virtue and the main vice of human cognition, a good choice would be *cognitive miserliness*. This feature of the mind is both desirable and inevitable, as it is neither cognitively beneficial nor feasible to constantly switch to reflective mode. At the same time, miserliness is perhaps the main obstacle for critical moral thinking, and the main aspect rendering the mind vulnerable.

The problem is that there is a permanent trade-off between labor and leisure in cognitive control (Kool and Botvinick 2014). Reflection is hard; intuition is cheap. As with other combinations of goods, thinkers gravitate towards the most highly valued point on their budget line of possible labor/leisure combinations. But the incentives aren't symmetrical, because in most cases, we can externalize the costs of bad, intuitive thinking. The benefits, however, accrue almost exclusively to those who indulge in miserly processing, who can consume extra cognitive leisure at the expense of the common good. This is a classic collective action problem, and it holds especially true in cases of moral cognition, where the subject matter is almost always *other people's* failings.

This means that in general, people won't be motivated to engage in critical Type III thinking. Speaking in terms of individual preferences, intuitive override is mostly instrumentally irrational, while defaulting to intuition pays off. But even if this were not so, there would be a problem, because it seems fair to ask who, if Type III (in cooperation with Type II) is supposed to initiate override of Type I, is in charge of initiating Type III?[11] The whole account seems to be built on the sands of infinite regress. The only answer to this objection I can think of is that it is simply correct. There *is* a regress problem here, which is that when it comes to initiating critical thinking, no one watches the watchmen. This is why all too often, reflection goes wrong or doesn't happen at all. This is simply the reality human thinkers have to work with.

I have argued above that there are plenty of ways in which reflective Type III thinking can be activated and supported. Among them are an intuitive feeling of error, debunking arguments, turning defensive reasoning inward, instilling intellectual humility and providing scaffolding through improving, or at least protecting, people's mental environment. Unfortunately, there are at least as many ways in which the initiation of critical moral reflection can fail.

Many think that social reasoning (intersubjective reasoning with others) will help facilitate intuition override.[12] Some even argue that reasoning is a social enterprise all the way down (Mercier and Sperber 2017). And there may be sound evolutionary reasons for this: given how strongly human life depends on successful communication, it seems plausible that the primary function of reasoning would be argumentative.

The ability to construct conscious inferences plays a role in persuading others more than in the atelic pursuit of the truth (Mercier and Sperber 2011).

This seems like a natural idea. How do people initiate intuitive override? By taking hints from others, who *are* motivated to challenge their interlocutors' beliefs. Like other forms of competition, this can have beneficial effects. People are guided, as if by an invisible hand, to contribute to the overall epistemic good. One person may be biased, but two biased persons may be impartial. Minus times minus equals plus, so that two homologous biases cancel each other out. However, there is no guarantee that this will work, or that it won't have the opposite result.

For instance, research on the "backfire effect" suggests that sometimes, being confronted with critical challenges to one's intuitive moral beliefs can make things worse. Nyhan and Reifler (2010; cf. Wood and Porter 2016) found that when one's moral – or, more precisely in this case: politically motivated – beliefs are corrected, people can become more confident in their beliefs. In one study, subjects were given statements by politicians (here: an excerpt from a speech by then-President of the US George W. Bush on the presence of weapons of mass destruction in post 9/11 Iraq). In the experimental condition, they subsequently received corrective information from the Duelfer Report, clarifying that this statement was, in fact, incorrect. It is one thing to find that participants identified as conservative were more likely to agree with Bush's statement. However, conservatives who received corrective information from the report were actually *more* likely to believe in the existence of WMDs in Iraq before US invasion. Social reasoning can make override more difficult.

There is another way in which the social structure of cognition can be responsible for Type III failure. Conformity effects make critical thinking and intuitive override difficult, which has been studied in a moral version of the famous Asch Paradigm. Kundu and Cummins (2013) gave subjects standard, Trolley-style moral dilemmas to judge. Some of these dilemmas are known to elicit high ratings of permissibility for the action they propose; some are known to yield very low-permissibility ratings. However, when subjects were confronted with atypical judgments made by instructed experimental confederates, their judgments would also start to lean more towards the atypical side. For instance, the mean permissibility ratings for low-permissibility transgressions, averaged across three vignettes, moved from 3.23 to 4.37 on a 7-point scale. Here, too, socially cooperative cognition distorts individual competence in moral judgment.

Critical moral reflection crucially depends on learning from past mistakes. Identifying past mistakes can help subjects store information on what's true or false, justified or unjustified, which can play a role in the future detection of the need for intuition override. Past mistakes sharpen the feeling of error, which is important for initiating Type III override. But this process, too, faces formidable obstacles. One of them is "ethical amnesia" (Kouchaki and Gino 2016).[13] When subjects are asked to recall past actions, their memory of unethical deeds is less vivid and specific. Participants who cheated on a coin-toss task also had less clear and accurate memories of their cheating two weeks later. This local form of amnesia may result from the discomfort that unethical behavior engenders.

Another source of Type III failure is due to structural epistemic oppression. Such *epistemic injustice* (Fricker 2007) comes in two forms: *hermeneutical* injustice robs people of the resources to understand or articulate the harms they suffer, *testimonial* injustice denies someone the status of counting as a credible source of information. One interesting example for an epistemically oppressive practice is so-called gaslighting (Abramson 2014), which is about contaminating another person's metacognitive abilities. By subtly inducing an ongoing sense of unreliability regarding one's own epistemic capacities, an individual's reflective capacities can become so allergized as to become untrustworthy. These practices are designed, intentionally or not, to undermine the critical thinking capacities of disadvantaged individuals or groups.

In the context of Type III failure, I also need to mention moral dumbfounding again: Haidt suggests that moral dumbfounding shows that reasoning doesn't produce moral judgments. Rather, intuitions bias the reasoning process in various infelicitous ways. Triple process theory interprets dumbfounding differently, namely as the breakdown of intuitive override in cases where people feel very strongly about an issue. This effect can become even more dramatic when people regard the reasons which are supposed to make them reconsider their judgment as dubious (see my discussion above). Clearly, however, moral dumbfounding does point towards an extremely widespread way in which critical thinking fails. In many cases, people defend, rather than scrutinize, their moral beliefs.

Perhaps the main source of Type III intervention failure is the so-called feeling of rightness that comes attached to many intuitive beliefs. This feeling is the flipside of the feeling of wrongness discussed above, and it is especially likely to be present in cases of moral judgment, whose emotionally charged character frequently makes it viscerally compelling. Thompson, Turner and Pennycook (2011; see also Thompson and Johnson 2014) suggest that this feeling of rightness is a metacognitive device that determines, to an important extent, how likely a subject is to engage reflective override.

What they found was that when the initial feeling of rightness is stronger, people take less time to rethink their intuitions, are less likely to reconsider them, and are thus less likely to give a normatively correct response.[14] This last point is indeed crucial, and will play an important role in my discussion of the normative implications of triple process moral psychology below. What I will suggest is that we have good reason to think that the output generated by Type III processing will lead to an improvement in the *quality* of people's moral judgments. And since, in the case of moral judgment, increased reflective cognition is correlated with a more progressive moral outlook, this insight can be used to construct a partial vindication of progressive moral judgments.

The problem with critical thinking is that the obstacles to it are self-disguising. In a way, this is just a restatement of the notorious Dunning-Kruger effect, applied to the case of moral judgment (Kruger and Dunning 1999, Dunning et al. 2003). People who lack critical thinking competence are also, and therefore, less likely to realize that they lack critical thinking competence. People who are bad at intuition override are also bad at seeing its point.

In order to capture the phenomenon of self-reinforcing Type III failure, Quassim Cassam has coined the useful term of *stealthy* intellectual vices (Cassam 2015). Intellectual vices are the flipside of reflective critical thinking dispositions. They include not just closed-mindedness and obtuseness, but also prejudice, conformity, and intellectual vanity. Some intellectual vices are, by their very nature, harder to detect than others. This makes override of intuitions generated on the basis of such dispositions, or backed up by their operation, especially hard. Stealthy vices are self-hiding: they "evade detection by those who have them" (Cassam 2016, 20). Being careless doesn't necessarily stand in the way of detecting that you are careless, as there may be some aware of their carelessness among the careless; but being closed-minded or cognitively arrogant may well stand in the way, in and of themselves, of coming to know that you are closed-minded or arrogant. It seems such stealthy vices can only be detected with the help of others. But then again, such vices will make it harder for me to take other people's assessment of my intellectual character into serious consideration.

Generally speaking, Type III failure seems to come in three varieties (de Neys and Bonnefon 2013): *storage* failure, *monitoring* failure, and *inhibition* failure. Necessary intuition override can remain undetected because subjects lack the ability to retrieve the formal knowledge required for override; they may show poor performance with regard to the detection of potential need for override and thus insufficient epistemic vigilance; or, finally, they may suffer from motivational problems that make it difficult for them to recruit their stored knowledge even after successful monitoring to prevent the default response generated by Type I from becoming full-fledged belief.

## Individual differences in moral judgment

One of the key pieces of evidence in support of the triple process account comes from individual differences in cognitive performance.

Remember that Triple Process Theory delineates algorithmic Type II processing from reflective Type III thinking to a large extent by looking at which parts of people's cognitive machinery explain which kind of performance. Here, it turned out that there are real, measurable differences between mere cognitive ability – the ability to generate, sustain, and manipulate decoupled representations in a way that recruits working memory, aka consciously controlled reasoning – and the critical thinking dispositions that initiate controlled reasoning. It also turned out that the latter are dissociable from the former.

In the case of moral judgment, this means that the crucial thing to look at is how individual differences in reflective thinking dispositions affect the formation of moral judgments. This is important because, for all we know, if critical thinking played no role whatsoever in moral judgment, there would be no reason to think that moral reasoning – which would then be exclusively the domain of Type II processing – would ever alter people's moral intuitions. When left unchecked by Type III dispositions, Type II would resort to its spin doctor role of producing rationalizations of moral gut reactions, rather than to second-guess them.

Issues of *timing* may be crucial for whether or not override is carried out successfully – or initiated at all (de Neys and Bonnefon 2013).[15] Importantly, this question can shed light on how *fundamental* the observed individual differences in critical thinking ability are. If these differences manifest fairly late in the reasoning process, this may suggest that performance differences are not due to the fact that there are two natural kinds of people such as biased and unbiased ones. Instead, most instances of override failure may be due to a "late state" divergence separating unbiased from biased individuals not in terms of what they know (storage failure) or become aware of (monitoring failure), but which otherwise identical responses they end up inhibiting.

These individual differences manifest in moral cognition. In line with the dominant dual process paradigm, there are studies suggesting that individual differences in working memory capacity influence moral cognition (Moore, Clark and Kane 2008). Now I have emphasized earlier (in part II) that working memory is precisely not what is essential for critical thinking, except as a tool with which it is carried out. Such studies crucially omit to address the issue of just what it is that makes subjects recruit their working memory capacity to process the information presented to them in various moral dilemmas to begin with. Here, it is important to emphasize that it is not incidental that the moral judgment tasks that typically form the basis of psychological studies of moral cognition use so-called moral *dilemmas* as prompts. In order to engage working memory, there needs to be some sort of tension that stands in need of resolution, which acts as an external scaffold for internal critical thinking dispositions. A moral judgment task with a simple, obvious solution involving no conflict triggers no WMC engagement (McGuire et al. 2009).

There is substantial evidence that individual differences in cognitive dispositions affect decision-making more generally (Phillips et al. 2016), for instance when it comes to risk assessments or procrastination. In the case of moral judgment, there are essentially two ways in which the effect of individual differences in reflective thinking on moral judgment can be tested: either by artificially inducing critical thinking in an experimental set-up, or by looking at existing critical thinking differences and how they affect moral beliefs.

The first option was pursued by Paxton, Ungar and Greene (2012) in a study I mentioned earlier. One of the experiments they did had subjects complete the *Cognitive Reflection Task* before responding to typical moral trade-offs such as the following:

> John is the captain of a military submarine traveling underneath a large iceberg. An onboard explosion has caused the vessel to lose most of its oxygen supply and has injured a crewman who is quickly losing blood. The injured crewman is going to die from his wounds no matter what happens.
>
> The remaining oxygen is not sufficient for the entire crew to make it to the surface. The only way to save the other crew members is

for John to shoot dead the injured crewman so that there will be just enough oxygen for the rest of the crew to survive.

(165)

Here, the idea is that completing the CRT will prime subjects to be more reflective and prepared to engage in intuition override. What they found was that subjects who had been induced to think critically about their intuitions gave more so-called utilitarian responses than subjects who first responded to the moral vignettes and then had to complete the CRT. In many moral dilemmas, the utilitarian option happens to be the counterintuitive one. Accordingly, this suggests that artificially induced individual differences in reflective dispositions affect moral judgment in the direction of intuition override.

The second option – existing reflective differences between subjects – has been studied by Pennycook et al. (2014). To gauge differences in critical thinking ability, they asked subjects to complete the CRT and a base-rate neglect task. Subjects were then asked to make moral judgments about Haidt's consensual incest scenario and the following famously endearing vignette from the world of paraphilic cuisine:

A man goes to the supermarket once a week and buys a dead chicken. But before cooking the chicken, he has sexual intercourse with it. He then cooks it and eats it in the privacy of his own home.

It turns out that there are very strong correlations between people's reflective cognitive dispositions – their willingness to detect the need for intuitive override and initiate it – and the degree of moral wrongness attributed to the actions described in the two stories just mentioned.

One possible explanation for this finding is that critical thinking in general is hostile to certain moral values and not others. Pennycook et al. found that a more strongly analytic cognitive style is negatively and positively correlated, respectively, with so-called binding and individualizing moral values such as respect for traditions, patriotism and loyalty, carnal purity, and respect for authority, as opposed to autonomy, helpfulness, or individual rights. From a triple process perspective, it is important to note raw cognitive ability – i.e. algorithmic Type II processing – made only a marginal difference to participants' moral judgment when cognitive style was controlled for

(Pennycook et al. 2014, 201). This suggests that it really is about critical thinking and not just the ability to engage in conscious reasoning as such that affects people's moral views.

These studies thus support the view, defended at length later on, that critical thinking selectively yields progressive, non-conservative moral views. Since (moral) beliefs arrived at via reflective dispositions to seek out more information, second-guess one's intuitive beliefs, consider alternative viewpoints, avoid myside bias, weigh evidence fairly and adjust one's credences accordingly are likely to be epistemically superior to beliefs which are formed on the basis of rough-and-ready Type I processes, this amounts to a (partial) vindication of some form of progressive moral outlook.

## Executing override: crystallized mindware

Individual differences in critical thinking dispositions do not fall from the sky. In many cases, these dispositions require some form of cognitive implementation. This implementation is done by *moral mindware*.

First, let me explain the role that ordinary, non-moral mindware plays in triple process theory. Here is some useful terminology to provide an even richer account of the content of the reflective system III. So far, I have focused on the critical thinking dispositions that detect the need for and monitor intuition override in the face of resistance from the miserly System I. Stanovich (2011) refers to these reflective tendencies as the "fluid" part of rationality (in analogy to fluid intelligence). This part of rationality is described as "fluid" because it consists of cognitive capacities that are generally applicable across a wide range of tasks: need for cognition, cognitive diligence or avoiding myside bias are cognitively useful in all domains of thinking.

Fluid rationality is complemented by *crystallized* rationality: stored features of the cognitive system that can be retrieved from memory. *Crystallized rationality* refers to the acquired knowledge structures that enable subjects to carry out intuition override when doing so would be difficult or impossible without the requisite cognitive tools.

The components of crystallized rationality are called *mindware*. Its primary function is to equip the algorithmic Type II with the means to carry out the override, the need for which has been identified by the fluid critical thinking components of Type III. Here, we can distinguish between mindware that promotes such override and mindware that undermines it. More precisely: so-called crystallized *facilitators* will improve the chances of successful (i.e. correct) intuition override, whereas crystallized *inhibitors* worsen those chances.

Importantly, neither of these components has an effect on the likelihood that override will or won't be *initiated*. An individual's mindware determines whether, once the need for a sequence of override has been detected by reflective Type III dispositions, Type III will have the actual cognitive tools at its disposal to successfully carry out such override. Moral mindware thus plays a crucial role in explaining Type III failure: it can be missing (mindware gaps), beneficial (crystallized facilitators) or detrimental (crystallized inhibitors).

Let me provide a brief overview of the components of fluid rationality – people's critical thinking dispositions – to really drive home the contrast with crystallized rationality. The major critical thinking dispositions are:

- Avoiding miserly processing
- Avoiding myside thinking
- Avoiding susceptibility to irrelevant context/framing effects
- Flexibility: open-minded thinking/avoiding dogmatism
- Valuing truth and reason (the "Master Rationality Motive")
- Need for cognition: tendency to seek information, enjoy thought, and fully process information
- Objective reasoning
- Tendency to seek consistency
- Self-control skills/prudent temporal discounting
- Emotional regulation[16]

These dispositions play an enormously important role in facilitating competent moral judgment: without them, subjects' underdeveloped distrust in their own intuitions would make it virtually impossible for them to detect the need for and initiate intuition override. They'd be stuck with the intuitions they happen to have, and would use their capacity of conscious reasoning almost exclusively to rationalize rather than question them.

I would like to note again that the critical thinking dispositions mentioned above blur the distinction between the epistemic and the moral. Many, if not most, epistemic virtues are already rife with moral content, and the other way around (open-mindedness, willingness to consider different perspectives and avoid myside bias, resistance to dogmatism, etc.). Adopting and cultivating these reflective Type III traits has substantive moral consequences. Many moral beliefs are incompatible with holding the above dispositions, because these beliefs are inherently in conflict with the propensity to consider opposing points of view, reason consistently, ignore morally irrelevant features, appreciate evidence, and remain open-minded.

As important as the above repertoire of Type III processing is, reflective dispositions to engage in critical thinking and intuition override will frequently remain ineffective if a subject lacks the knowledge structures required to carry out such override. This is where the need for functioning mindware arises.

In many cases, the mindware acting as a set of crystallized facilitators for rational thought has to be *learned*. When it isn't, this can result in *mindware gaps*. Consider base-rate neglect. Probabilistic thinking is notoriously difficult to do well on the basis of intuitions alone. For instance, people routinely make mistakes about estimating the likelihood of a state of affairs – such as whether or not a person has been infected with a disease – because they ignore the fact that given a sufficiently low base rate, even a reliable test can deliver a surprisingly high amount of false positives, such that the positive results of a test that almost never "misses" a disease (i.e. has a low false negative rate) is still of very little evidential value regarding whether or not it actually obtains. This is a problem of missing mindware, because the thinking strategies that allow individuals to identify this error have to be acquired.

The fluid critical thinking dispositions that constitute one part of System III are domain-general, and can be put to equally good use in moral and non-moral thinking. In the case of crystallized facilitators and inhibitors, we can give examples that apply specifically to the domain of moral judgment.

Consider, for instance, the so-called golden rule. Many have noted that it yields disastrous moral advice when followed to the letter. It generates far too many false positives (it may imply, for instance, that it is wrong for a judge to convict a criminal because she wouldn't want to be convicted herself) and false negatives (it has no resources for ruling out many obviously immoral acts as morally wrong). It is thus neither necessary nor sufficient for classifying acts as right or wrong. However, when understood as moral mindware to facilitate critical moral thinking, clumsy heuristics like the golden rule can start to make sense. They are not to be taken literally, but are easy-to-use perspective taking devices that can lead to a reduction in self-centered thinking virtually everyone is naturally prone to. Since this reduction is morally desirable but difficult to achieve otherwise, the golden rule can be seen as a useful piece of facilitating mindware.

When it comes to gaps in moral mindware, the inability to introspectively detect inconsistent moral beliefs – pairs of moral judgments whose difference in content is due to a morally irrelevant difference – should rank close to the top in terms of priority (Campbell and Kumar 2012, Campbell 2017). Singer (2011) urges his readers to see that not saving a drowning child so as not to ruin one's expensive suit (call this option A) is morally on a par with buying an expensive suit instead of giving the money to famine relief (call this option B). Greene wants to make the case that diverting a trolley to save five workmen at the expense of one (option A) is the same, morally speaking, as pushing the fat man in front of the trolley (option B). And Huemer (2013) wants us to accept that locking criminals in your basement and coercively collecting payments from your neighbors for this service *just is* what the state does. In all of these cases, the suggestion goes, we are not treating like cases alike.

I use these examples merely for the purpose of illustration. One does not have to agree substantively with the moral judgments the episodes of reasoning sketched above end up suggesting. The issue is not that this or that case does really exhibit moral inconsistency. The problem is that such moral inconsistencies exist, and that there is no readily available piece of mindware available to correct for them.

Now consider, as an example for *contaminated* mindware, zero-sum bias (Meegan 2010, Różycka-Tran, Boski and Wojciszke 2015). Zero-sum games are games in which one player's losses are the other player's gains. In zero-sum games, mutual or indeed merely unilateral gains are impossible. This leads to a kind of "fixed pie" thinking according to which what I win, you lose. This bias plays out in moral judgment, too. Some people earnestly seem to think that widespread enhancements in cognitive ability – think boosts to intelligence, memory, mental arithmetic, and so on – would benefit no one in the long run. Kean Birch (2005), for instance, holds that:

> Crucially though, despite the fact that parents may want their children to be "intelligent," where all parents want this any beneficial effect is nullified. On the one hand intelligence could be raised to the same level for all or, alternatively, intelligence could be raised by the same amount for all. In either case no one actually benefits over anyone else.

Don't even bother vaccinating you children. Once everyone does it, nobody will be any better off!

Folk economics, too, is shot through with zero-sum thinking (Brennan and Jaworski 2015, 172ff.). If China becomes rich, it must be at Western nations' expense; if some people are talented and innovative, poor people will suffer (see Heath 2009 and, relatedly, Krugman's famous *Ricardo's Difficult Idea*). Such zero-sum thinking may have been a useful moral heuristic in a context in which mutually advantageous win-win interactions were rare or non-existent. Under modern circumstances, however, this bias continues to contaminate people's thinking – with all sorts of pernicious effects.[17]

A third category I would like to add is what could be referred to as *reflexive* mindware. It is arguably impossible to counteract many of the problems resulting from mindware gaps or contaminated mindware without being aware of their existence and what causes them. Reflexive mindware concerns a continued awareness of one's critical thinking deficits and the mindware problems that animate them. This does not necessarily entail that simply by being aware of them, we can get rid of our biases. Far from it. In many cases, however, it can at least mean that we can engineer our physical or social environment – for instance, by removing certain types of information from job applications, or by inviting experts to panel discussions – to curb their manifestation.

Earlier I mentioned the important role the external environment plays for virtually all cognitive operations. To what extent does the ability to override faulty intuitions, engage in critical thinking and use appropriate moral mindware depend on external support and institutional scaffolding? Here, too, we have little reason to say that epistemic dispositions/ critical thinking traits and crystallized cognitive structures have to be "in the head" – a more externalist account is also promising, according to which certain social structures which institutionalize that people's intuitive beliefs continue to be challenged and revised, and which make available the tools to enact such challenging and revising – such as science, an education system, a properly functioning media, political discourse in cafés and parliaments, a thriving art scene, or a dense urban environment, may be equally important for facilitating reflective override.

This social externalist perspective establishes close ties between empirically informed metaethics and political philosophy. If rational and competent moral judgment is based on intuitive override, which is promoted by epistemic dispositions which, in turn, are often crystallized in social institutions, then a case can be made for maintaining those institutions. Consider another example from the culinary world: of course, digestion goes on in the digestive system including the stomach, colon, and other internal organs. But that doesn't mean that healthy digestion does not depend on external scaffolding, such as chopping, cooking, roasting, fermenting, and so forth. Our digestive systems are "scaffolded" by such externalized practices of preparing and cooking food (Sterelny 2010). Similarly, our practice of critical moral thinking, which to a certain extent undeniably goes on in the head and draws on internal mental resources, heavily depends on external institutional scaffolding. When this scaffolding breaks down, our critical thinking abilities become severely impaired, because they are deeply socially sustained.

## Intuition activation

It would perhaps make most sense to describe the function of reflective Type III cognition as one of general intuition management rather than mere override, because critical thinking isn't always in the business of curtailing problematic moral intuitions. Sometimes, the problem isn't that people have an intuition that it would be better for them not to have, but that they *lack* an intuition that it would be useful for them to have. Critical thinking is not just in charge of intuitive override, but also intuition *activation*.

The need for intuition activation becomes clear when considering one of the main rationales for override again. The processes generating our moral intuitions can often be *hypersensitive*. What people are up to when they make moral judgments is to make a deontic selection: of all the actions they are confronted with and need to render a verdict about, they want to distinguish the wrong from the right ones. In order to get at this target attribute of rightness/wrongness, they often pick up on clumsy proxies such as what pleases or repels them, rather than to focus on all and only the strictly speaking morally relevant features of the situation.

Disgust-based moral intuitions are a particularly pertinent example here.[18] Due to its evolutionary heritage as part of our extended immune system, disgust reactions were selected for their role in avoiding contamination by pathogens and/or toxins. However, there is a characteristic cost/benefit asymmetry here, which is that the benefits of not ingesting contaminated food typically greatly outweigh the costs of foregoing a non-contaminated nutritional opportunity. This means that disgust evolved as a trigger happy *better safe than sorry* mechanism with a high tolerance for generating an enormous amount of false positives: things that are ruled out as to-be-avoided (i.e. disgusting) even though they are actually perfectly fine (i.e. objectively uncontaminated). Due to its inherent malleability, the disgust mechanism could later be coopted to police social norms as well (Kelly 2011). This mission creep can become morally pernicious, as disgust-based moral intuitions end up classifying way too many act types and tokens as wrong, and people as the moral enemy. Hence the need for reflective override.

But often, the problem isn't the presence of a flawed intuition that needs to be overridden as much as the absence of a legitimate intuition that needs to be activated. One of the processes that is responsible for such *hyposensitive* intuitions is empathy. Empathy is supposed to make us care about other people, but it is often woefully inadequate in doing so. The "shallow pond" thought experiment can again be used as an illustration of empathy's stinginess and the resulting inconsistency in our moral intuitions about the duty to help the needy.

The limits of empathy can be studied fairly precisely. Here, the phenomena of pseudo inefficacy (Västfjäll, Slovic and Mayorga 2015) and compassion fade (Västfjäll et al. 2014) stand out. Compassion fade refers to the diminishing marginal empathy people experience with an increasing number of suffering people. In fact, people's feelings of concern – measured in terms of their willingness to make a fictional or real donation – seem to be inversely proportional to the magnitude of the problem: caring is strongest for one identifiable individual, after which it steeply declines. Pseudo inefficacy is the effect that people become less inclined to help one suffering child when they are presented with two children, only one of which can be helped, rather than one child they can help. Note, of course, that in both cases they *can* help the same number of children.

As with disgust, there may be an evolutionary rationale for this stinginess. Caring for others is expensive in time and resources, and so a gene-centered view of evolution (Dawkins 2016) would predict the motivation to be concerned about others would be restricted to a rather tight circle of family and friends. Here, critical thinking is called for to recognize the inconsistency in our responses and generate, most likely by recruiting affective assistance, an intuition that doesn't depend on a morally irrelevant difference.

In the next section, I will explain in greater detail the role of "crystallized moral mindware" in bringing about such a result. For now, let me emphasize that moral mindware is of particular importance for the activation of such "missing" intuitions. Crystallized intuitions can help facilitate the detection of a need for intuition generation because they alert the cognitive system to possible incongruences, and supply a corresponding feeling of error. In yet another modification of the ball/bat problem, Trémolière and de Neys (2014) found that prior intuitions can help subjects detect believability problems. Consider this structurally analogous version of the problem:

A Ferrari and a Ford together cost $190000. The Ferrari costs $100000 more than the Ford. How much does the Ford cost?

Here, the intuitive response cued by the numbers ($90000) conflicts with many[19] people's implicit knowledge of the respective prices of Fords. This, in turn, activates their Type III critical thinking dispositions which detect the need for and initiate Type II reasoning.[20]

Likewise, moral mindware in the form of prior moral intuitions can help detect believability problems in the construal of moral scenarios. For whatever reason, many people seem inclined to shift at least some of the responsibility for an incident of rape onto the victim. Once one has a steady grasp on the concept of *victim blaming*, however, it can become easier to second-guess this tendency and enable people to question the moral intuitions and responsibility attributions resulting from this. Here, the override of a flawed moral intuition is complemented by the activation of a more appropriate one, which would have been considerably more difficult with a less generously equipped moral judgment toolkit.

## Mindware and moral error

Both the failure to override a faulty moral intuition and the failure to initiate a legitimate one can be sources of moral error. But this is not all there is to it: one of the best features of the triple process framework is the nuanced account it offers of the sources of cognitive error. This account can inform our thinking about *moral* error as well, and potentially help to avoid its most egregious instances.

The concept of moral mindware goes a long way with regard to understanding moral error from a triple process perspective. Stanovich provides an extensive list of mindware gaps, contaminated mindware and facilitating mindware in his account of triple process theory (2011). One of the most important tasks of the triple process account proposed here is to come up with an analogous list of mindware problems for the case of moral cognition. A tentative suggestion for such a list is what I aim to provide here.

Due to the haphazard imprint the environment of evolutionary adaptedness has left on our ancestors' minds, it is difficult to derive such a list from first principles. The best we can do may be to identify some common and normatively urgent errors in moral cognition, and to find overarching categories to helpfully sort them into separate groups. This, at any rate, is what Stanovich's typology seems to be after (see Table 3.1).

The two broadest categories of cognitive error are cognitive miserliness and mindware problems. In the first case, people make mistakes because they default to the autonomous/preattentive processing mode of the intuitive mind. This can happen because they either do not recognize the need for intuition override at all, which may be due to an overly drowsy feeling of error and underdeveloped epistemic dispositions to engage in reflective thinking, or because they do recognize the need for override, but fail to initiate, monitor, or execute it properly.

The latter problem, in particular, can be exacerbated by the second broad category of thinking errors. Mindware problems also come in two forms: it can be missing or contaminated. Stanovich's list is long: as we have seen, mindware gaps can concern probabilistic thinking (base-rate

*Table 3.1* Stanovich's Typology of Cognitive Errors (adapted from Stanovich 2009a)

| Type | Source | Examples |
| --- | --- | --- |
| The Cognitive Miser | Default to the Autonomous Mind Serial Associative Cognition with Focal Bias Override Failure | |
| Mindware Problems | Mindware Gaps | Probability Knowledge Importance of Alternative Hypotheses Domain-Specific Knowledge Structures Lay Psychological Theory |
| | Contaminated Mindware | Lay Psychological Theory Evaluation-Disabling Strategies Egocentric Processing Domain-Specific Knowledge Structures |

neglect), logical inference (belief-bias effects), principles of scientific reasoning (disconfirmation, correlation vs. causation), or economic errors (sunk costs, externalities). Contamination can occur in the same domains, and then some. Superstitious thinking, overconfidence, dogmatism, or excessive trust in one's gut reactions all undermine optimal performance in various cognitive tasks.

In what follows, I will sketch a typology of *moral* judgment errors and discuss a variety of relevant examples. Let me emphasize in advance that for most of the examples that I am about to give, it does not matter whether or not one agrees with the substantive moral judgments employed in them. I happen to think that these examples are sound, but they are first and foremost used for the purpose of illustration. Readers who disagree with the chosen cases can substitute their own favorite mindware problems. All I am trying to do here is to justify the important role of an account of moral error in terms of override failure, mindware gaps and contaminated mindware for critical thinking within a triple process theory of moral judgment.

## *Default to intuition*

As in the case of non-moral judgment, the cognitive miser looms large as a source of moral error. Moral judgment is difficult to do (well). In order to arrive at a well-informed evaluation of even a simple everyday situation, one needs to appreciate an abundance of possible considerations of ambiguous relevance and weight. It thus remains tempting for leisurely minds like ours to cognitively replace the property of moral wrongness with only contingently related but easier-to-process features such as an action's disgustingness or sheer unfamiliarity.

Cass Sunstein (2005b) aims at something similar with his account of moral heuristics. His "catalogue" (535) of faulty processing shortcuts contains, among other things, failures of cost-benefit analysis, problematic punitive reactions, or ill-conceived intuitions about nature and the cosmos. Interestingly, Sunstein is an inadvertent example for how being in possession of the reflexive mindware of knowing about how moral heuristics can make our intuitions misfire offers only weak protection against them. For instance, in his discussion of Michael Sandel's critique of pollution and the moral offensiveness of emissions trading, he accuses Sandel of relying on a heuristic according to which one should not be permitted to engage in wrongdoing for a fee. Sunstein admits that this heuristic works for some cases, as there are purportedly "no tradable licenses for rape, theft, or battery" (537).

Sunstein's own heuristics misfire here, too, however. Boxers, shop owners or sex workers will be able to testify to the fact that there comes a point at which the amount of money one receives makes one at least indifferent between the remuneration and the otherwise undesired outcome of being beaten up, having something taken away from someone or having sex with a stranger one isn't attracted to. In all of these cases, people can become willing to do certain things for a fee that it would be seriously wrong to do to them without the pecuniary manufacturing of consent. The license for theft *is* tradable. Such trade is called "selling stuff."

The cognitive miser is perhaps never more miserly than when she gauges how acceptable or objectionable something is in terms of its familiarity. The concept of status quo bias refers to an unjustified preference for whatever happens to be the case at the time. This bias can inform people's moral assessment of a variety of policy issues ranging from medical interventions to environmental protection. People's preference for the status quo also makes them engage in asymmetrical assessments of costs and benefits with regard to changing something vs. leaving things as they are. For any given proposed change to the status quo, only the possible costs and disadvantages are salient, whereas for the status quo, the benefits engender the most attention. This makes status quo bias one of the most pervasive and harmful biases of all.

The power of the autonomous mind is at its most striking display when intuition enlists analytic forms of processing to cook up arguments for its inherent smartness. Perhaps most famously, Leon Kass has defended the idea that there is a "wisdom of repugnance" (Kass 1997). In some cases, the fact that a feeling of moral horror is beyond articulation or rational defense is supposed to be a virtue, rather than a vice. Default to intuition would thus be morally and epistemically preferable even in cases in which the superiority of automatic cognition is beyond comprehension, and indeed *contrary* to the available evidence. This is the slave of the passions defending its own terms of employment.

In reality, moral intuitions have an important role to play. For purely pragmatic reasons alone, it would be impossible to engage in critical monitoring of one's intuitions all the time. However, it remains true that many characteristically modern moral, social, and political problems simply do not allow for (correct) intuitive solutions. Unfortunately, these problems are precisely the ones where, due to their inherent difficulty, the temptation to default to intuition is strongest. Intuition override thus remains a rare and precious thing.

## Override failure

In some cases, the need for override is detected by a subject's Type III critical thinking dispositions. Nevertheless, the risk remains that such override either isn't initiated or, if it is initiated, that it is not executed properly. The key thing to realize is that unlike in the case of moral error due to intuitive processing, the main culprit for moral error due to override failure is not System I, but System II. This is because when System II is activated, but System III remains uninvolved, moral reasoning is likely to make moral judgments *worse* (Hindriks 2014 and 2015). Conscious moral reasoning without support by critical thinking dispositions and crystallized moral mindware yields self-serving rationalizations rather than competent moral reflection.

In short: override failure is the road to moral disengagement. Generally, override failure due to moral disengagement is a great test case for the theoretical value of Triple Process theory, because moral disengagement is quite literally made possible by System II processing. When unchecked by the reflective third type, moral reasoning will find a way to bring one's moral intuitions in line with one's interests. The phenomenon of moral disengagement shows that in and of itself, System II does not care about the distinction between proper reasoning and rationalization. Disengagement is facilitated by System II when it is left unmonitored by Type III (see Figure 3.3).

Uncritical moral reasoning facilitates override failure by allowing subjects to twist facts and moral standards to excuse or redescribe wrongful

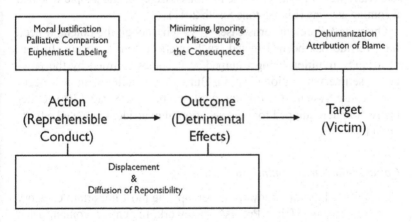

*Figure 3.3* Moral Disengagement (adapted and modified from Bandura 1996, 265)

conduct. Bandura (1996) has developed the most helpful typology of targets of rationalization and disengagement. In most cases, morally wrong action will consist of three elements: the action (*conduct*), the outcome (*effects*), and the people affected (*victim*). Typically, when an individual harms another, there will on some level be an intuitive appreciation that what the individual has done is wrong, according to some standard of moral evaluation. Unfortunately, human moral reasoners are capable of extraordinarily sophisticated forms of reasoning when it comes to maintaining the appearance of goodness.

Wrongful conduct can be given a moral justification in terms of a higher social value (such as honor or the common good); it can be favorably compared to other people's bad deeds (whataboutism *avant la lettre*); and it can be relabeled to seem more acceptable ("ethnic cleansing" for "genocide" or "mass murder"; "separate but equal"; "men's rights"). The bad outcome of one's reprehensible actions can be declared insignificant (minimization), non-existent (ignorance), or misunderstood (misconstrual). Those who had to suffer the consequences can be blamed for bringing it on themselves (e.g. the Nazis had to defend themselves against the conspiratorial efforts to annihilate the Aryan race orchestrated by international Jewry) or dehumanized: Native Americans, or black Africans, or Sinti and Roma, or Jews, or Mexicans, or Catholics, or Muslims, or Women, or [. . .] are really either subhuman scum that doesn't deserve the same kind of moral consideration or indeed disgusting and dangerous vermin that has to be exterminated. All of this leads to a convenient diffusion of responsibility where insignificant cogs in the wheel were mere bystanders when things that really weren't that bad in the first place were done to people who had it coming anyway (Livingstone Smith 2011).

Override failure concerns cases in which, though the potential need for override has been detected, such override fails to occur. Instead of a faulty intuition being trumped, it becomes fortified by the powers of self-serving rationalization. But override failure can also occur not because System II is running wild, but because System III is either badly or underequipped for the execution of override. Let me take these up in turn.

### Contaminated moral mindware

Contaminated moral mindware is perhaps the most important category of moral error in a Triple Process framework. In general, contaminated mindware concerns crystallized knowledge structures that decrease, rather than improve, the quality of moral judgment. Such mindware can persistently generate toxic moral intuitions or distort otherwise unproblematic cognitive dispositions in a morally undesirable direction.

In the case of non-moral cognition, Stanovich refers to contaminated mindware as a set of "crystallized inhibitors" of rational thought. Here, various expressions of myside bias and egocentric processing are perhaps the most obvious examples. In the case of moral judgment and reasoning, the crystallized inhibitors contaminating subjects' mindware can either be deeply entrenched or superficial and acquired. In what follows, I will focus, firstly, on contaminated mindware that inhibits progressive moral developments in the direction of egalitarian inclusion. Secondly, I will discuss a few recent cases of problematic moral thinking from the public realm to highlight the diagnostic usefulness of the approach developed here.

Consider, for instance, the famous ingroup/outgroup distinction. Evolutionary psychology supports the view that humans are inevitably groupish (Haidt 2012, Greene 2013). People's innate moral dispositions automatically lead them to carve up the social world in terms of friend and foe. Expansions of the moral circle are almost always hard-won and fragile. Depending on which salient features of a person this disposition latches on to, the results can range from sports hooliganism to standard anti-immigration sentiment to outright xenophobia. Now in principle, it makes sense for us to distinguish between those entities that deserve moral consideration and those that do not. But more often than not, the ingroup/outgroup distinction functions as a piece of contaminated crystallized mindware that inhibits the accurate drawing of those boundaries. This can – and routinely does – have all kinds of harmful downstream effects, as when people oppose pro-immigration policies even though these generally constitute a win-win situation.[21]

Above, I have described moral disengagement as a type of override failure. One of the main techniques of moral disengagement I mentioned was to picture the victims of one's wrongful conduct in a dehumanizing light. This dehumanization is typically facilitated by pernicious ideologies and essentialist thinking (Livingstone Smith 2011). Such exclusivist ideologies are the ingroup/outgroup distinction on steroids. People are always sensitive to the possibility of outgroup threat. Under certain conditions of (real or imagined) economic turmoil, political instability or even mere cultural decadence and fatigue, the possibility of such threats can be spun into a viscerally compelling scapegoating narrative according to which parasitic and/or treacherous and/or hostile groups threaten to undermine the wholesomeness and wellbeing of the community (Buchanan and Powell 2016). In most cases, these exclusivist ideologies are backed up by seemingly reputable historical or biological pseudoscientific theories allegedly showing that the threatening outgroup is either deficient or secretly all-powerful or – believe it or not – both.

To add insult to injury, negative stereotypes vis-à-vis outgroups are magnified by a supraindividual version of the fundamental attribution error. Negative aspects of outgroups are judged to be due to internal characteristics, whereas positive observations are explained in terms of contingent situational factors. For ingroup members, the reverse is true: positive features are welcomed as essential characteristics; negative ones are excused as incidental situational deviations (Hewstone 1990).

Exclusivist and discriminatory attitudes, though extremely important, are not the only types of contaminated moral mindware. Examples for bad moral judgment abound. Take zero-sum thinking again. In an unholy alliance of this tendency with status quo bias and technophobia, a recent newspaper article argues – despite its *admitted* benefits – against the externalization of pregnancy through artificial wombs on grounds of its inegalitarian effects. If affluent women can afford to technologically bypass the risks of natural pregnancy, this will only come at poorer women's expense. For the latter, it becomes impossible to escape the newly created "reproductive class."[22] This moral objection fails to explain, however, why benefits to some people must come at the expense of others. Traditionally, reproductive technologies such as contraception are – once they have become familiar and the panic has faded away – almost universally welcomed as being hugely beneficial particularly for the poor and marginalized.

The concept of human dignity is another moral wolf in sheep's clothing. Few people who travel in the moral vocabulary of dignity are condemned for embracing a vague and atavistic moral sledgehammer. In most cases, wanting to preserve human dignity involves tremendous reputational benefits. On the other hand, some people have made the case that intuitions grounded in dignity are holding us back (Pinker 2008 and 2015) by encumbering us with a set of inflexible moral prohibitions that forestall the adoption of beneficial biomedical or institutional innovations such as CRISPR/Cas9 genome editing or assisted suicide.

Intuitions about sanctity and bodily purity form an important part of people's moral repertoire, and are defended by many as a proper foundation of morality on a par with disapproval of harm and support of rights and fairness. This may or may not be true (my guess is that it is not); in many cases, however, purity-based moral intuitions make people oppose common sense regulations such as programs designed to improve the lives of drug addicts. In one recent US case, this has led an Indiana county to abandon its needle exchange program – with predictably regrettable consequences for public health. Nevertheless, one county commissioner Rodney Fish is quoted as saying that "[i]t was a moral issue with me. I had severe reservations that were going to keep me from approving that motion [. . .] I did not approach this decision lightly. I gave it a great deal of thought and prayer. My conclusion was that I could not support this program and be true to my principles and my beliefs."[23] All of this may, in fact, be true. But it is also beside the point, because whether one's thoughts and principles are worth staying true to lies at the heart of moral reasoning as much as figuring out what they entail.

Another recent article reports that China is about to introduce an app-based social credit system that allows individuals and the government to keep track of people's trustworthiness.[24] This system – which it will apparently become mandatory for every natural and legal person to participate in by 2020 – would monitor people's financial, criminal, legal, political, commercial, and even their private behavior to increase social capital and mutual trust in people and institutions. Naturally, many people are alarmed, and are quick to condemn this as nightmarishly intrusive, and they may well be right. However, this judgment seems to be based almost entirely on comparing the *benefits* of the current, informal system of judging people's trustworthiness with the *costs* of the suggested replacement. The judgment is made on the basis of miserly processing that fails to engage in full decoupling of all relevant alternatives. In order to have any real purchase on the value of the policy, one would have to compare the benefits *and costs* of the current arrangement with the costs *and benefits* of the alternative. Here, it seems not obviously better to judge other people in terms of what are essentially markers of social class – the way people dress, speak, move about, groom their finger nails or judge art – to gauge their trustworthiness. Imagine that what is now a possible future were in fact reality, and the system we now have would be proposed as a progressive reform. This would likely be considered horrific as well. Again, I am not suggesting that the new system is indeed better, only that our intuitive rejection of its merits is based on substantially underpowered thinking.

In a recent book, Fiske and Rai (2014) argue that most forms of violence are justified, that is: people justify them as a matter of empirical fact – in terms of some moral purpose. On their account, violent behavior is typically not a form of social deviance due to breakdowns of self-control, but seen as a virtuous form of honoring moral norms and values. People punish, mutilate, kill, rape, torture, and go to war because doing so is thought to play an important role in regulating the moral realm of interpersonal relations.

People also frequently base their moral judgments on socially contingent symbolic considerations. One doesn't have to be a naïve market fundamentalist to think that the current situation, in which thousands of people die every year due to organ shortages and thousands more spend the better part of their week hooked up to dialysis machines is untenable, and indeed embarrassing for developed nations.[25] Yet most people are categorically opposed to the idea of a market in organ donations, even if most (or perhaps all) of their objections – most notably, the risk of exploiting the poor – could be straightforwardly regulated away (Brennan and Jaworski 2015).[26] The objection seems to be primarily grounded in the suspicion that the buying and selling of organs somehow "commodifies" them, and that this is incompatible with their inherent value. Here, too, we can see how certain forms of "symbolic" thinking encourage resistance towards mutually beneficial, and indeed life-saving, forms of cooperation.

In all of these cases, it is likely that crystallized inhibiting mindware – primitive punitive reactions, misguided conceptions of responsibility and desert, unfounded assumptions about purity and cleanliness, status quo bias, biological essentialism, the "golden age" fallacy, and simple mistakes of availability and representativeness – winds up contaminating our moral judgment.

I do not mean to suggest that all mistakes in moral judgment are due to missing or contaminated moral mindware. Oftentimes, people get it wrong simply because they don't have accurate information, or they are careless, or mean, or just plain irrational. What I do wish to suggest, however, is that studying moral error in terms of critical thinking mindware can be a productive way of looking at the issue. Properly identifying the source of error is the first step towards remedying it.

Let me emphasize again that one need not agree with the substantive moral judgments in the above examples for contaminated mindware, just like one need not agree, substantively, with the examples I gave for improvements in moral judgment after initiating override through reflective critical thinking dispositions. What I am trying to illustrate is that moral judgment is only insufficiently understood without these concepts, and that the nature of moral cognition and reasoning is best described not in terms of System I and System II, but in terms of a network of automatic and controlled cognition whose interaction is managed by a third type of critical thinking which is in charge of monitoring intuitions and initiating override when necessary.

## Mindware gaps

Mindware doesn't have to be contaminated to produce unjustified moral judgments. It can also be *absent*. I have already mentioned a lack of resources for intuition activation in the form of low empathy towards strangers, unidentifiable victims or large groups. Many more striking examples can be drawn from folk economics. Like folk physics (McCloskey 1983), folk economics is riddled with confusions and magical thinking. It takes considerable training to become able to override, or perhaps even get rid of, these faulty intuitions. For instance, most people experience an extremely strong moral revulsion towards price gouging (Zwolinski 2008), and consider it unfair to raise prices in response to increased demand (Kahneman, Knetsch and Thaler 1986). Here, the underlying logic of price signals and their combined epistemic and motivational effects is a missing piece of mindware that is counterintuitive and thus difficult to appreciate.

Stanovich (2009b, 129ff.) shows that some pieces of mindware, such as Bayesian reasoning, need to be explicitly taught and learned to figure in people's override toolkit. This goes for some moral mindware as well. Consider status quo bias again. A preference for whatever happens to be actual is very hard to detect or get rid of. But it can, at least in principle, be diagnosed and overridden. Bostrom and Ord (2006) propose what they call the "reversal test" to counteract status quo bias: if you are against some proposed change $x$ – for instance, cognitive enhancements or improvements to health and longevity – consider a symmetrical change $y$ in the *opposite* direction. If one opposes both increases *and* decreases to current levels of, say, intelligence, then one may be subject to status quo bias. This test is a piece of mindware that has to be acquired, and its use practiced.

My argument, then, is this: firstly, there are certain cognitive features or processes for which there is overwhelming evidence that they constitute epistemic improvements, and lead to increases in the *quality* of people's thinking. Secondly, epistemic improvements along those lines, when applied to the moral domain, unequivocally lead to changes in a certain direction, namely, more progressive moral and political judgments. To be sure, this argument does not provide conclusive *proof* that progressive moral and political judgments are epistemically superior to non-progressive ones. But they establish a steep burden of proof for those who wish to deny this claim. One would have to show why and in what sense the moral domain is special such that uncontroversial epistemic improvements, though they *do* have a significant measurable effect on moral judgment, and thus do *not* leave moral judgments merely unaffected, should be normatively neutral, even though these effects point into one clear progressive direction of further moral and political liberalization. My argument is thus a *vindicating* argument for progressive moral beliefs: it shows that such beliefs are robustly correlated with cognitive processes which we otherwise do not hesitate to classify as epistemically superior.

### A typology of moral judgment errors

The resulting typology of moral judgment error looks something like this (see Table 3.2).

This typology is obviously not exhaustive, but it gives a rough idea of some of the main ways in which moral judgment can go wrong.

*Table 3.2* Moral Error from a Triple-Process Perspective

| Type | Source | Examples |
| --- | --- | --- |
| Default to Intuition | Status Quo Bias | Anti-Enhancement Attitudes, Beliefs about "Human Nature" |
| | Attribute Substitution | Confusing rightness with naturalness, frequency, etc. |
| | Affective Reactions | Disgust, Resentment, Envy |
| Override Failure | Moral Disengagement | Euphemistic Descriptions Misconstrual of Consequences Victim Blaming Rejection of Responsibility |
| | Missing Reflective Dispositions | Dogmatism, Faith in Intuition |
| Activation Failure | Empathy | Pseudo inefficacy Compassion Fade |
| | Moral Dumbfounding | Closed-Mindedness |
| Mindware Gaps | Hermeneutic Injustice | Missing Vocabulary for Self-Understanding ("Sexism," "Ableism") |
| | Economic Reasoning | Prices, Opportunity Costs, Supply and Demand, Comparative Advantage |

| Type | Source | Examples |
|---|---|---|
| Contaminated Mindware | Ingroup/Outgroup Thinking | Dehumanization, Scapegoating, Essentialist Thinking, Perceptions of Outgroup Threat |
| | Intuitions about Sanctity/Purity | Bioethical Intuitions Intuitions about Dignity Drug Prohibitions |
| | Punitive Intuitions | Retributivism, The "War on Drugs" |
| | Zero-Sum Thinking | Anti-Immigration Attitudes |
| | Economic Intuitions | Anti-Market Attitudes |

Let me mention two more observations if only for the sake of completion. Stanovich himself focuses on cases where higher cognition performs better than Type I. But it ain't necessarily so. Two further categories that need to be added are about cases where the opposite is true. Firstly, there can be too little (rather than too much) input from System I. Such cases are familiar from Damasio's work in how emotional impairments (i.e. a lack of somatic markers) can be detrimental for cognition and decision-making. Moreover, Type II and III processing can make people's judgments worse, too (Wilson and Dunn 1989, Wilson and Schooler 1991). My plea for the importance of executive override should not be mistaken for a naïve form of rationalist triumphalism.

## Rationalist pessimism

Quite the opposite, in fact. My account entails that competent moral judgment is extremely difficult, and depends on cognitive resources that are always in short supply. Rational moral judgment is real, but rare. I refer to this as *rationalist pessimism*. But is it true? And if it is, what should be done about it?

There are a few options. We could become simple pessimists, accepting the fact that even though there is such a thing as rational moral judgment, only very few people, on very few occasions, will do it properly. And even when they do, it is worth mentioning that effect sizes for the impact of critical thinking aren't very large (Phillips et al. 2016).

Another piece of evidence that people are actually fairly bad at forming justified moral views about policy options comes from the phenomenon of "motivated numeracy" (Kahan et al. 2017). Even people who are equipped with the required mindware become really bad at using it when confronted with ideologically inconvenient information. It is not an overstatement to say that in all likelihood, our moral mindware is full of gaps. A lot of it should also likely be considered contaminated, and should be counted among the crystallized inhibitors rather than facilitators.

Many of the standard vignettes in the moral psychology literature – trolley dilemmas, the dumbfounding vignettes, and so on – can be seen as moral critical thinking tasks akin to the ball/bat problem. When looking at subjects' performance, we can see that they are likely lacking in both important components of System III: in the fluid critical thinking dispositions that detect the need for and initiate override, and in the moral reasoning mindware that allows such override to be carried out by the algorithmic Type II.

In many politically and morally important areas, such as immigration or economics, System I isn't just badly equipped to give the right answer. It is *positively biased* in favor of the wrong answer. Ingroup/outgroup thinking distorts our views on immigration, and various economic fallacies and intuitions about tribal fairness trap us in a variety of economic fallacies.

A further problem is that the proper functioning of intuitive processing often depends on implicit learning mechanisms. However, many of the most pressing moral issues – emergencies, local or global – are either unique, or at least novel, unprecedented, and inherently messy, so that System I judgments are particularly ill-equipped to deal with them as they don't receive any useful feedback about one-off judgments.

Politics, economics, and social morality are topics where, due to the inherent unintuitiveness of these fields that come with modern social conditions, critical thinking is most needed. But the "cognitive miser" problem makes critical thinking always at least *somewhat* costly to the individual subject. This means that people have, by default, a standing incentive *against* critical thinking. This incentive is then exacerbated by the fact that in morality, as in politics, uncritical subjects do not bear the (full) cost of their erroneous ways. When the personal consequences of unreflective, miserly thinking are practically nil, cognitive misers' demand for irrationality increases.

The Triple Process account offers a form of rationalism with a pessimistic twist. The aforementioned distribution of incentives further supports this pessimism. The situation is that when it comes to the very topics that most need to be considered critically and reflectively, the costs of bad, and indeed reckless and dangerous, judgment and decision-making can be almost fully externalized. Given that people have existing preferences to hold political and moral beliefs that make them "feel good" inside, this basically guarantees that people will have strong incentives to think badly and incompetently where it matters most. Since this applies to essentially everyone, the (relatively high) costs and the (relatively low) benefits of critical thinking about political and social morality create a classic tragedy of the commons where everyone consumes more unreflective thinking than the collective can handle. Just consider, for a brief moment, the objective seriousness and difficulty of issues such as the death penalty, health care or immigration, and the frivolity with which people go about forming moral and political beliefs on them.

Triple Process moral psychology shows that counterintuitive, progressive moral judgments are likely to be preferable to intuitive moral beliefs. This is because modern societies tend to be hostile environments for intuitive processing, which either make necessary cues unavailable or provide misleading cues that lead to misfiring. But note that in order to get to these normative implications, I need not argue that issues that require reflective processing tend to be frequent, or even the norm. In fact, I believe that in *most* situations, our heuristics, and even our biases, still serve us reasonably well. What's more important is that the *significant* issues tend to be the ones which can only properly be addressed with critical thinking such as how our political, civil, social, legal, and economic institutions should be run. These issues may be rare, but tragically, they tend to be the ones where we are especially motivated to go with our gut, because they tend to be so emotionally charged. This is another way in which the Triple Process account is a form of rationalistic pessimism: reason is real, but the obstacles to its effective enactment are very powerful, and indeed self-reinforcing.

Another possibility is for us to become *meliorists*: the Triple Process account may support the idea that people's cognitive traits ought to be enhanced whenever possible. I am in principle sympathetic to this solution, but what if cognitive traits cannot be enhanced, or not without substantial costs, or not yet? This question leads to an interesting, potentially *elitist* implication of my view. It is that the vast majority of people, namely those that do not have the cognitive skills and traits to make competent moral judgments, or have no access to the information required to do so, should be discouraged from making any moral judgments at all. We tend to think that everyone is entitled to make moral judgments. But given the serious harms that judging others can impose on the so judged, most people should perhaps refrain from making moral judgments, leaving the practice of moral thinking to whoever has what it takes to make them competently.

Consider the fact that moral cognition often consists in making moral judgments about other people, and that such judgments frequently have harmful consequences for them: it can lead to the marginalization of certain groups or the ostracism of individuals. In fact, that's part of their point. But it is morally wrong to engage in irresponsible and risky behavior that negatively affects others on the basis of unjustified beliefs or careless reasoning. Therefore, it does not seem implausible that most people should at least engage *in far less* moral judgment than they currently do.

Unfortunately, it may be the case that we simply *cannot* refrain, either at all or as easily, from making moral judgments. Joshua Knobe cites evidence suggesting that we are "moralizers through and through" (2010). He argues that a) virtually all of our cognition is suffused with moral influence and that b) this influence is inaccessible to our conscious awareness. It may be that carefully designed studies of the kind social psychologists and experimental philosophers conduct can reveal some of that influence and its workings to us. In that case, and when certain special and demanding conditions are met, it may be that we can put the knowledge regarding the influence of moral contamination to reflexive use and discount that influence. But this is presumably very rare.

A final powerful argument for pessimism about moral judgment draws on the principle of *behavioral symmetry* (Freiman 2017, Brennan and Buchanan 2008). When theorizing about institutions, for instance, we shouldn't justify government intervention in the market by assuming that people are selfish in the market but saintly in government. One needs a special reason to justify such asymmetrical behavioral assumptions. The reasons why government intervention is needed are also the reasons why it may not work. Likewise, it is a striking fact that when theorizing about morality and ethics, philosophers readily admit that people are prone to all sorts of immoral behavior in their actions. In fact, one of the main reasons offered for why we need to engage in moral judgment and reasoning in the first place is that people are weak-willed, ignorant, vicious, and sometimes downright evil. And if they are not, then decades of moral psychology have taught us that getting people to behave *as if* they were evil is ridiculously easy. But all of a sudden when moral *judgment* is concerned, people are assumed to be fair-minded, diligent, and impartial. Why would this be so? Competent moral judgment is difficult, unpleasant, and time-consuming. People have every incentive to be self-serving and biased in their moral thinking, or perhaps especially there. One shouldn't justify the need for moral judgment in terms of people's shortcomings and then assume those shortcomings away in people's moral judgment. If people are nice, moral judgment isn't needed. If it is needed at all, then there is no guarantee that people will do it *well*.

## After metaethics

Triple Process moral psychology renders the main options in traditional metaethics *scientifically obsolete*.

The realism/anti-realism distinction comes first. Doesn't the Triple Process account, with all its talk of correctness of moral judgments and moral progress, presuppose moral realism? I think the answer is: no. We can study various norms of reasoning – about probability, logic, mathematics – without thereby presupposing anything about the metaphysics of these domains, and without assuming that there are facts about probability or validity that these norms are answering to. They are simply norms of reasoning. Likewise, there are norms of moral reasoning, and moral mistakes arise when these norms of moral reasoning are violated. Moreover, the triple process account can offer a plausible evolutionary rationale for why certain forms of reasoning and judgment formation are likely to be unreliable – they have been selected for different contexts, and are no longer fitting under "hostile" modern conditions. If anything, the triple process account shows just how much of interest can be said about moral error and its sources without saying anything about moral ontology at all.

Secondly, there is the sentimentalism/rationalism distinction. To a large extent, empirically informed metaethics still operates within the basic distinction between sentimentalist and rationalist accounts of moral judgment (Prinz 2016). Triple Process Moral Psychology shows that the distinction between sentimentalism and rationalism about moral judgment is outdated. Moral judgment does not depend on emotion *or* reason – as if that dichotomy ever made much sense to begin with! – but on an integrated network of intuitive, algorithmic, and reflective types of cognitive processing. Affectively neutral and affectively hot processes can, just like automatic and controlled ones, be found across the board.

Thirdly, the Triple Process account of moral judgment and reasoning developed ultimately undermines the distinction between cognitivism and non-cognitivism about moral judgment. Moral cognition is based, not on belief *or* desire, but on automatic, algorithmic, and reflective cognition. The functional profiles of these states – mind-to-world or world-to-mind direction of fit – are all over the place. Intuitions have propositional content, but are also affectively valenced; critical thinking dispositions define epistemic goals, but are fundamentally in the business of getting at the truth; moral mindware consists of crystallized knowledge structures that implement practical cognitive strategies. From this perspective, the cognitive/non-cognitive distinction seems crude at best and confused at worst. Some of it is affective, some of it is automatic, some of it is conscious. It's *all* cognition.

Moral judgment is a largely intuitive enterprise, but that doesn't make it non-rational, or place it outside of the space of reasons. It becomes part of the space of reasons because of the way moral intuitions are monitored by reflective capacities, overridden by conscious thinking, and shaped by moral mindware. This cooperation of intuition, conscious processing and critical thinking may seem haphazard and kludgy at times, but it's what we have to make do with. It is how finite beings reason.

## Notes

1  Indeed, Shea and Frith (2016) posit "type zero" as a fifth type.
2  On the possibility of vindicating arguments, see Sauer 2018, forthcoming. Like debunking arguments, vindicating arguments do not provide direct support for the truth of their conclusions. Debunking arguments are undercutting defeaters; likewise, vindicating arguments merely show that, before looking at its content, a given judgment has comparatively better epistemic credentials. This is all I wish to establish in what follows.
3  I am indebted to Heath (forthcoming) for these references.
4  See Widerquist and McCall (2017).
5  Elsewhere, I refer to this type of argument as a form of obsoleteness debunking; see Sauer (forthcoming).
6  It should be noted early on that overriding one's moral intuitions does *not* always improve their quality. See Białek and Handley (2013) on this.
7  For an interesting alternative explanation, see Wright and Baril (2011).
8  This is largely due to the fact that many authors do not operate within the framework proposed here, and simply collapse type II and type III together.
9  The acronym WEIRD stands for *W*estern *E*ducated *I*ndustrialized *R*ich *D*emocratic.
10  See Pennycook et al. (2014) for evidence that people's willingness to engage in critical thinking predicts reduced judgments of wrongness about conservative issues. In Sauer (2015), I show that reflective thinking preferentially undermines "conservative" moral foundations, but leaves progressive moral intuitions intact. Check out Yilmaz and Saribay (2017), Saribay and Yilmaz (2017) and Napier and Luguri (2013) for the connection between cognitive style and individualism. Importantly, analytic thinking enhances liberal foundations independent of prior political orientation. See also Pennycook and Rand (manuscript).

11 Thanks to Pauline Kleingeld for discussions on this point. I should stress that here I am not talking about a logical regress. Rather, this "regress" is due to certain contingent cognitive limitations.

12 Thanks to Mark Alfano for pressing me on this.

13 Kouchaki and Gino actually refer to the phenomenon as *un*ethical amnesia, which is more correct but less elegant.

14 Note, however, that there was a *negative* correlation between rethinking time and task accuracy.

15 See also Pennycook, G., Fugelsang, J. A., & Koehler, D. J. (2015).

16 This list paraphrases the one found in Stanovich 2011, 195 for this; see also Stanovich (2009a).

17 Somin, I. (2016, July 24). Identity Politics and the Perils of Zero Sum Thinking. Retrieved from www.washingtonpost.com/news/volokh-conspiracy/wp/2016/07/24/prejudiceand-the-perils-of-zero-sum-thinking/?utm_term=.edc520ff5dac; Lombrozo, T. (2014, September 22). Being Good Isn't Zero Sum. Retrieved from www.npr.org/sections/13.7/2014/09/22/350519216/being-good-isnt-zero-sum; Harford, T. (2017, August 25). Trump, Bannon, and the lure of zero-sum thinking. Retrieved from www.ft.com/content/381f5888-88b0-11e7-bf50-e1c239b45787

18 On the moral relevance of disgust, see Sauer (2012c), Plakias 2013, and Kumar (2017).

19 A significant gender difference was found in this study, likely reflecting men's far greater average interest in cars and their compensatory effects.

20 Annoyingly, the authors don't give away what the correct solution to the problem is, but my calculations suggest that it is $45.000.

21 Cowen, T. (2017, November 15). The earlier age of mass migration also brought political backlash. Retrieved from http://marginalrevolution.com/marginalrevolution/2017/11/earlier-age-massmigration-america-also-brought-political-backlash.html

22 Glosswitch (2017, November 14). Artifical wombs could liberate elite women at the expense of the reproductive classes. Retrieved from https://www.newstatesman.com/politics/feminism/2017/11/artificial-wombs-could-liberate-elite-women-expense-reproductive-classes

23 Lopez, G. (2017, October 20). An Indiana county just halted a lifesaving needle exchange program, citing the Bible. Retrieved from www.vox.com/policy-and-politics/2017/10/20/16507902/indiana-lawrencecounty-needle-exchange

24 Botsman, R. (2017, October 21). Big data meets Big Brother as China moves to rate its citizens. Retrieved from http://www.wired.co.uk/article/chinese-government-social-credit-score-privacy-invasion

25 Postrel, V. (2009, July) . . . With Functioning Kidneys for All. Retrieved from www.theatlantic.com/magazine/archive/2009/07/with-functioning-kidneysfor-all/307587/

26 If I recall correctly, in Germany, even altruistic, non-commercially motivated kidney donations to strangers are illegal.

# References

Abramson, K. (2014). Turning up the lights on gaslighting. *Philosophical Perspectives, 28*(1), 1–30.

Alfano, M. (2011). Expanding the situationist challenge to responsibilist virtue epistemology. *The Philosophical Quarterly, 62*(247), 223–249.

Alfano, M. (2016). *Moral psychology: An introduction.* Polity.

Alfano, M., Iurino, K., Stey, P., Robinson, B., Christen, M., Yu, F., & Lapsley, D. (2017). Development and validation of a multi-dimensional measure of intellectual humility. *PloS One, 12*(8), e0182950.

Althaus, S. L. (2003). *Collective preferences in democratic politics: Opinion surveys and the will of the people.* Cambridge University Press.

Appiah, A. (2008). *Experiments in ethics.* Cambridge, MA, Harvard University Press.

Ariely, D. (2008). *Predictably irrational.* New York, HarperCollins: 20.

Bandura, A., Barbaranelli, C., Caprara, G. V., & Pastorelli, C. (1996). Mechanisms of moral disengagement in the exercise of moral agency. *Journal of Personality and Social Psychology, 71*(2), 364.

Berker, S. (2009). The normative insignificance of neuroscience. *Philosophy & Public Affairs, 37*(4), 293–329.

Białek, M., & De Neys, W. (2016). Conflict detection during moral decision-making: Evidence for deontic reasoners' utilitarian sensitivity. *Journal of Cognitive Psychology, 28*(5), 631–639.

Białek, M., & Handley, S. J. (2013). Overriding moral intuitions – Does it make us immoral? Dual-process theory of higher cognition account for moral reasoning. *World Academy of Science, Engineering and Technology, International Journal of Social, Behavioral, Educational, Economic, Business and Industrial Engineering, 7*(5), 1153–1156.

Birch, K. (2005). Beneficence, determinism and justice: An engagement with the argument for the genetic selection of intelligence. *Bioethics, 16*, 12–28, 24.

Bostrom, N., & Ord, T. (2006). The reversal test: Eliminating status quo bias in applied ethics. *Ethics, 116*(4), 656–679.

Brennan, G., & Buchanan, J. M. (2008). *The reason of rules.* New York, Cambridge University Press.

Brennan, J. F., & Jaworski, P. (2015). *Markets without limits: Moral virtues and commercial interests*. Routledge.

Buchanan, A., & Powell, R. (2016). Toward a naturalistic theory of moral progress. *Ethics, 126*(4), 983–1014.

Campbell, R. (2017). Learning from moral inconsistency. *Cognition, 167*, 46–57.

Campbell, R., & Kumar, V. (2012). Moral reasoning on the ground. *Ethics, 122*(2), 273–312.

Caplan, B. (2007). *The myth of the rational voter: Why democracies choose bad policies*. Princeton University Press.

Cassam, Q. (2015). Stealthy vices. *Social Epistemology Review and Reply Collective, 4*(10), 19–25.

Cassam, Q. (2016). Vice epistemology. *The Monist, 99*(2), 159–180.

Clark, A. (2008). *Supersizing the mind: Embodiment, action, and cognitive extension*. Oxford University Press.

Clark, A., & Chalmers, D. (1998). The extended mind. *Analysis, 58*(1), 7–19.

Damasio, A. R. (1994). *Descartes' error: Emotion, rationality and the human brain*. London, Penguin.

Darwall, S., Gibbard, A., & Railton, P. (1992). Toward fin de siecle ethics: Some trends. *The Philosophical Review, 101*(1), 115–189.

Dawkins, R. (2016). *The selfish gene*. Oxford University Press.

de Neys, W., & Bonnefon, J. F. (2013). The 'whys' and 'whens' of individual differences in thinking biases. *Trends in Cognitive Sciences, 17*(4), 172–178.

Doris, J. M. (2002). *Lack of character: Personality and moral behavior*. New York, Cambridge University Press.

Doris, J., & Stich, S. (2005). "As a Matter of Fact: Empirical Perspectives on Ethics." In: F. Jackson and M. Smith (eds.). *The oxford handbook of contemporary philosophy*. New York City, NY, Oxford University Press: 114–152.

Dunning, D., Johnson, K., Ehrlinger, J., & Kruger, J. (2003). Why people fail to recognize their own incompetence. *Current Directions in Psychological Science, 12*(3), 83–87.

Eidelman, S., Crandall, C. S., Goodman, J. A., & Blanchar, J. C. (2012). Low-effort thought promotes political conservatism. *Personality and Social Psychology Bulletin, 38*(6), 808–820.

Evans, J. S. B. (2008). Dual-processing accounts of reasoning, judgment, and social cognition. *Annual Review of Psychology, 59*, 255–278.

Evans, J. S. B. (2009). "How Many Dual-Process Theories Do We Need? One, Two, or Many?" In: J. Evans and K. Frankish (eds.). *In two minds: Dual processes and beyond*. New York City, NY, Oxford University Press: 33–55.

Evans, J. S. B., & Stanovich, K. E. (2013). Dual-process theories of higher cognition: Advancing the debate. *Perspectives on Psychological Science, 8*(3), 223–241.

Fessler, D. M. T., Pisor, A. C., & Holbrook, C. (2017). Political orientation predicts credulity regarding putative hazards. *Psychological Science, 28*(5), 651–660.

Fiske, A. P., & Rai, T. S. (2014). *Virtuous violence: Hurting and killing to create, sustain, end, and honor social relationships*. New York, Cambridge University Press.

Fodor, J. A. (1983). *The modularity of mind: An essay on faculty psychology*. Cambridge, MA, MIT Press.

Frederick, S. (2005). Cognitive reflection and decision making. *The Journal of Economic Perspectives, 19*(4), 25–42.

Freiman, C. (2017). *Unequivocal justice*. Routledge.

Fricker, M. (2007). *Epistemic injustice: Power and the ethics of knowing*. Oxford University Press.

Gangemi, A., Bourgeois-Gironde, S., & Mancini, F. (2015). Feelings of error in reasoning – In search of a phenomenon. *Thinking & Reasoning, 21*(4), 383–396.

Gat, A. (2008). *War in human civilization*. Oxford University Press.

Gigerenzer, G. (2008). *Gut feelings: Short cuts to better decision making*. London, Penguin.

Gray, K., Schein, C., & Ward, A. F. (2014). The myth of harmless wrongs in moral cognition: Automatic dyadic completion from sin to suffering. *Journal of Experimental Psychology, 143*(4), 1600.

Greene, J. (2013). *Moral tribes: Emotion, reason, and the gap between us and them*. London, Penguin.

Greene, J. D. (2008). "The Secret Joke of Kant's Soul." In: W. Sinnott-Armstrong (ed.). *Moral psychology Vol. 3: The neuroscience of morality: Emotion, brain disorders, and development*. Cambridge, MA, MIT Press.

Greene, J. D. (2014). Beyond point-and-shoot morality: Why cognitive (neuro)science matters for ethics. *Ethics, 124*(4), 695–726.

Greene, J. D. (2017). The rat-a-gorical imperative: Moral intuition and the limits of affective learning. *Cognition, 167*, 66–77.

Greenspan, P. (2015). Confabulating the truth: In defense of "defensive" moral reasoning. *The Journal of Ethics, 19*(2), 105–123.

Guglielmo, S. (2018). Unfounded dumbfounding: How harm and purity undermine evidence for moral dumbfounding. *Cognition, 170*, 334–337.

Haidt, J. (2001). The emotional dog and its rational tail. *Psychological Review, 108*, 814–834.

Haidt, J. (2012). *The righteous mind: Why good people are divided by religion and politics*. London, Penguin.

Haidt, J., & Bjorklund, F. (2008). "Social Intuitionists Answer Six Questions About Moral Psychology." In: W. Sinnott-Armstrong (ed.). *Moral psychology. Vol. 2: The cognitive science of morality: Intuition and diversity*. Cambridge, MA, MIT Press: 181–217.

Haigh, M. (2016). Has the standard cognitive reflection test become a victim of its own success? *Advances in Cognitive Psychology, 12*(3), 145.

Hall, L., Johansson, P., & Strandberg, T. (2012). Lifting the veil of morality: Choice blindness and attitude reversals on a self-transforming survey. *PloS One, 7*(9), e45457.

Heath, J. (2009). *Filthy Lucre: Economics for people who hate capitalism*. New York, HarperCollins.

Heath, J. (2014a). *Enlightenment 2.0: Restoring sanity to our politics, our economy, and our lives*. New York, HarperCollins.

Heath, J. (2014b). Rebooting discourse ethics. *Philosophy & Social Criticism, 40*(9), 829–866.

Heath, J., & Anderson, J. (2010). "Procrastination and the Extended Will." In: Ch. Andreou and M. White (eds.). *The thief of time: Philosophical essays on procrastination.* New York City, NY, Oxford University Press, 233–252.

Heath, J. (forthcoming). "On the Scalability of Cooperative Structures." Remarks on G. A. Cohen, *Why Not Socialism?* Unpublished Manuscript.

Heath, J., & Hardy-Vallée, B. (2015). Why do people behave immorally when drunk? *Philosophical Explorations, 18*(3), 310–329.

Henrich, J., Heine, S. J. et al. (2010). The weirdest people in the world? *Behavioral and Brain Sciences, 33*(2–3), 61–83.

Hewstone, M. (1990). The 'ultimate attribution error'? A review of the literature on intergroup causal attribution. *European Journal of Social Psychology, 20*(4), 311–335.

Hindriks, F. (2014). Intuitions, rationalizations, and justification: A defense of sentimental rationalism. *The Journal of Value Inquiry, 48*, 195–216.

Hindriks, F. (2015). How does reasoning (fail to) contribute to moral judgment? Dumbfounding and disengagement. *Ethical Theory and Moral Practice, 18*(2), 237–250.

Hirstein, W. (2005). *Brain fiction: Self-deception and the riddle of confabulation.* Cambridge, MA, MIT Press.

Huemer, M. (2013). *The problem of political authority.* Palgrave Macmillan.

Huemer, M. (2016). A liberal realist answer to debunking skeptics: The empirical case for realism. *Philosophical Studies, 173*(7), 1983–2010.

Inbar, Y., Pizarro, D. A., & Bloom, P. (2009). Conservatives are more easily disgusted than liberals. *Cognition Emotion, 23*(4), 714–725.

Jacobson, D. (2012). Moral dumbfounding and moral stupefaction. *Oxford Studies in Normative Ethics, 2*, 289–316.

Johansson, P., Hall, L., Sikström, S., & Olsson, A. (2005). Failure to detect mismatches between intention and outcome in a simple decision task. *Science, 310*(5745), 116–119.

Johnson, E. D., Tubau, E., & De Neys, W. (2016). The doubting system 1: Evidence for automatic substitution sensitivity. *Acta Psychologica, 164*, 56–64.

Jost, J. T., Glaser, J., Kruglanski, A. W., & Sulloway, F. J. (2003). Political conservatism as motivated social cognition. *Psychological Bulletin, 129*(3), 339–375.

Kahan, D. M., Peters, E., Dawson, E. C., & Slovic, P. (2017). Motivated numeracy and enlightened self-government. *Behavioural Public Policy, 1*(1), 54–86.

Kahane, G. (2012). On the wrong track: Process and content in moral psychology. *Mind & Language, 27*(5), 519–545.

Kahane, G. et al. (2012). The neural basis of intuitive and counterintuitive moral judgment. *Social Cognition & Affective Neuroscience, 7*(4), 393–402.

Kahane, G. et al. (2015). "Utilitarian" judgments in sacrificial moral dilemmas do not reflect impartial concern for the greater good. *Cognition, 134*, 193–209.

Kahneman, D. (2000). A psychological point of view: Violations of rational rules as a diagnostic of mental processes. *Behavioral and Brain Sciences, 23*(5), 681–683.

Kahneman, D. (2003). A perspective on judgment and choice: Mapping bounded rationality. *American Psychologist, 58*(9), 697–720.

Kahneman, D. (2011). *Thinking, fast and slow.* Palgrave Macmillan.

Kahneman, D., Knetsch, J. L., & Thaler, R. (1986). Fairness as a constraint on profit seeking: Entitlements in the market. *The American Economic Review, 76*(4), 728–741.

Kahneman, D., Tversky, A. et al. (eds.). (1982). *Judgment under uncertainty: Heuristics and biases.* Cambridge, Cambridge University Press.

Kass, L. R. (1997). The wisdom of repugnance. *New Republic, 216*(22), 17–26.

Kelly, D. (2011). *Yuck!: The nature and moral significance of disgust.* Cambridge, MA, MIT Press.

Knobe, J. (2010). Person as scientist, person as moralist. *Behavioral and Brain Sciences, 33*(4), 315–329.

Kool, W., & Botvinick, M. (2014). A labor/leisure tradeoff in cognitive control. *Journal of Experimental Psychology: General, 143*(1), 131.

Koralus, P., & Alfano, M. (2017). "Reasons-Based Moral Judgment and the Erotetic Theory." In: Bonnefon J. F. and B. Tremoliere (eds.). *Moral inferences.* Psychology Press, Taylor & Francis.

Kouchaki, M., & Gino, F. (2016). Memories of unethical actions become obfuscated over time. *Proceedings of the National Academy of Sciences, 113*(22), 6166–6171.

Kruger, J., & Dunning, D. (1999). Unskilled and unaware of it: How difficulties in recognizing one's own incompetence lead to inflated self-assessments. *Journal of Personality and Social Psychology, 77*(6), 1121.

Kruglanski, A. W., & Gigerenzer, G. (2011). Intuitive and deliberate judgments are based on common principles. *Psychological Review, 118*(1), 97.

Kumar, V. (2017). Foul behavior. *Philosophers' Imprint, 17*(15), 1–17.

Kundu, P., & Cummins, D. D. (2013). Morality and conformity: The Asch paradigm applied to moral decisions. *Social Influence, 8*(4), 268–279.

Landy, J. F., & Goodwin, G. P. (2015). Does incidental disgust amplify moral judgment? A meta-analytic review of experimental evidence. *Perspectives on Psychological Science, 10*(4), 518–536.

Leslie, A. M. (1987). Pretense and representation: The origins of' theory of mind. *Psychological Review, 94*(4), 412.

Machery, E. (2014). In defense of reverse inference. *The British Journal for the Philosophy of Science, 65*(2), 251–267.

May, J. (2014). Does disgust influence moral judgment? *Australasian Journal of Philosophy, 92*(1), 125–141.

McCloskey, M., Washburn, A., & Felch, L. (1983). Intuitive physics: The straight-down belief and its origin. *Journal of Experimental Psychology: Learning, Memory, and Cognition, 9*(4), 636.

McGuire, J., Langdon, R. et al. (2009). A reanalysis of the personal/impersonal distinction in moral psychology research. *Journal of Experimental Social Psychology, 45*, 577–580.

Meegan, D. V. (2010). Zero-sum bias: Perceived competition despite unlimited resources. *Frontiers in Psychology, 1*.

Menary, R. (ed.). (2010). *The extended mind.* Cambridge, MA, MIT Press.

Mercier, H., & Sperber, D. (2011). Why do humans reason? Arguments for an argumentative theory. *Behavioral and Brain Sciences, 34*, 57–111.

Mercier, H., & Sperber, D. (2017). *The enigma of reason.* Cambridge, MA, Harvard University Press.

Moore, A. B., Clark, B. A., & Kane, M. J. (2008). Who shalt not kill? Individual differences in working memory capacity, executive control, and moral judgment. *Psychological Science, 19*(6), 549–557.

Nail, P. R., McGregor, I., Drinkwater, A. E., Steele, G. M., & Thompson, A. W. (2009). Threat causes liberals to think like conservatives. *Journal of Experimental Social Psychology, 45*(4), 901–907.

Napier, J. L., & Luguri, J. B. (2013). Moral mind-sets: Abstract thinking increases a preference for "individualizing" over "binding" moral foundations. *Social Psychological and Personality Science, 4*(6), 754–759.

Nichols, S., Kumar, S., Lopez, T., Ayars, A., & Chan, H. Y. (2016). Rational learners and moral rules. *Mind & Language, 31*(5), 530–554.

Nichols, S., & Stich, S. P. (2003). *Mindreading: An integrated account of pretence, self-awareness, and understanding other minds*. Oxford University Press.

Nickerson, R. S. (1998). Confirmation bias: A ubiquitous phenomenon in many guises. *Review of General Psychology, 2*(2), 175.

Nisbett, R. E., & Wilson, T. D. (1977). Telling more than we can know: Verbal reports on mental processes. *Psychological Review, 84*(3), 231–259.

Nisbett, R. E., & Wilson, T. D. (1978). The accuracy of verbal reports about the effects of stimuli and behavior. *Social Psychology, 41*(2), 118–131.

Nyhan, B., & Reifler, J. (2010). When corrections fail: The persistence of political misperceptions. *Political Behavior, 32*(2), 303–330.

Paxton, J. M., Bruni, T., & Greene, J. D. (2013). Are 'counter-intuitive' deontological judgments really counter-intuitive? An empirical reply to Kahane et al. (2012). *Social cognitive and affective neuroscience, 9*(9), 1368–1371.

Paxton, J. M., Ungar, L. et al. (2012). Reflection and reasoning in moral judgment. *Cognitive Science, 36*(1), 163–177.

Pennycook, G., Cheyne, J. A., Barr, N., Koehler, D. J., & Fugelsang, J. A. (2014). The role of analytic thinking in moral judgements and values. *Thinking & Reasoning, 20*(2), 188–214.

Pennycook, G., Cheyne, J. A., Barr, N., Koehler, D. J., & Fugelsang, J. A. (2015). On the reception and detection of pseudo-profound bullshit. *Judgment and Decision Making, 10*(6), 549.

Pennycook, G., Fugelsang, J. A., & Koehler, D. J. (2015). What makes us think? A three-stage dual-process model of analytic engagement. *Cognitive Psychology, 80*, 34–72.

Pennycook, G., & Rand, D. G. 2018. "Who Falls for Fake News? The Roles of Analytic Thinking, Motivated Reasoning, Political Ideology, and Bullshit Receptivity." Manuscript.

Pinker, S. (2008). The stupidity of dignity. *The New Republic, 28*, May 2008.

Pinker, S. (2015). The moral imperative for bioethics. *Boston Globe*, August 2015.

Plakias, A. (2013). The good and the gross. *Ethical Theory and Moral Practice, 16*(2), 261–278.

Poldrack, R. A. (2006). Can cognitive processes be inferred from neuroimaging data? *Trends in Cognitive Sciences, 10*(2), 59–63.

Pollock, J. (1987). Defeasible reasoning. *Cognitive Science, 11*, 481–518.

Prinz, J. (2016). "Sentimentalism and the Moral Brain." In: S. M. Liao (ed.). *Moral brains: The neuroscience of morality*. New York City, NY, Oxford University Press: 45–74.

Proust, J. (2013). *The philosophy of metacognition: Mental agency and self-awareness*. Oxford University Press.

Railton, P. (2017). Moral learning: Conceptual foundations and normative relevance. *Cognition, 167*, 172–190.

Richerson, P. J., & Boyd, R. (2005). *Not by genes alone: How culture transformed human evolution*. University of Chicago Press.

Royzman, E. B., Kim, K., & Leeman, R. F. (2015). The curious tale of Julie and Mark: Unraveling the moral dumbfounding effect. *Judgment and Decision Making, 10*(4), 296.

Różycka-Tran, J., Boski, P., & Wojciszke, B. (2015). Belief in a zero-sum game as a social axiom: A 37-nation study. *Journal of Cross-Cultural Psychology, 46*(4), 525–548.

Saribay, S. A., & Yilmaz, O. (2017). Analytic cognitive style and cognitive ability differentially predict religiosity and social conservatism. *Personality and Individual Differences, 114*, 24–29.

Sauer, H. (2012a). Morally irrelevant factors: What's left of the dual-process model of moral cognition? *Philosophical Psychology, 25*(6), 783–811.

Sauer, H. (2012c). Psychopaths and filthy desks: Are emotions necessary and sufficient for moral judgment? *Ethical Theory and Moral Practice, 15*(1), 95–115.

Sauer, H. (2015). Can't we all disagree more constructively? Moral foundations, moral reasoning, and political disagreement. *Neuroethics, 8*(2), 153–169.

Sauer, H. (2017a). *Moral judgments as educated intuitions*. Cambridge, MA, MIT Press.

Sauer, H. (2017b). "Between Facts and Norms: Ethics and Moral Psychology." In: B. Voyer and T. Tarantola (eds.). *Moral psychology: A multidisciplinary guide*. USA, Springer: 5–29.

Sauer, H. (2018). *Debunking arguments in ethics*. Cambridge University Press.

Schlenker, B. R., Chambers, J. R., & Le, B. M. (2012). Conservatives are happier than liberals, but why? Political ideology, personality, and life satisfaction. *Journal of Research in Personality, 46*(2), 127–146.

Schlosser, M. E. (2012). Free will and the unconscious precursors of choice. *Philosophical Psychology, 25*(3), 365–384.

Schnall, S., Haidt, J. et al. (2008). Disgust as embodied moral judgment. *Personality and Social Psychology Bulletin, 34*, 1096–1109.

Shea, N. J., & Frith, C. (2016). Dual-Process theories and consciousness: The case for 'type zero' cognition. *Neuroscience of Consciousness 1*(1).

Singer, P. (2011). *The expanding circle: Ethics, evolution, and moral progress*. Princeton University Press.

Sinnott-Armstrong, W., Young, L., & Cushman, F. (2010). "Moral Intuitions." In: J. Doris and The Moral Pscyhology Research Group (eds.). *The moral psychology handbook*. New York City, NY, Oxford University Press.

Slovic, P., Finucane, M. L., Peters, E., & MacGregor, D. G. (2002). "The affect heuristic." In: T. Gilovich, D. Griffin and D. Kahneman (eds.). *Heuristics and biases: The psychology of intuitive judgment.* New York, Cambridge University Press: 397–420.

Smith, D. L. (2011). *Less than human: Why we demean, enslave, and exterminate others.* St. Martin's Press.

Stanovich, K. E. (2005). *The robot's rebellion: Finding meaning in the age of Darwin.* University of Chicago Press.

Stanovich, K. E. (2009a). Distinguishing the reflective, algorithmic, and autonomous minds: Is it time for a tri-process theory? In: J. Evans and K. Frankish (eds.). *In two minds: Dual processes and beyond.* New York City, NY, Oxford University Press: 55–89.

Stanovich, K. E. (2009b). *What intelligence tests miss: The psychology of rational thought.* Yale University Press.

Stanovich, K. (2011). *Rationality and the reflective mind.* Oxford University Press.

Stanovich, K. E., & West, R. F. (2000). Individual differences in reasoning: Implications for the rationality debate? *Behavioral and Brain Sciences, 23*(5), 645–665.

Stanovich, K. E., & West, R. F. (2007). Natural myside bias is independent of cognitive ability. *Thinking & Reasoning, 13*(3), 225–247.

Stanovich, K. E., & West, R. F. (2008). On the relative independence of thinking biases and cognitive ability. *Journal of Personality and Social Psychology, 94*(4), 672.

Sterelny, K. (2010). Minds: Extended or scaffolded? *Phenomenology and the Cognitive Sciences, 9*(4), 465–481.

Sunstein, C. R. (2005a). *Laws of fear: Beyond the precautionary principle.* Cambridge University Press.

Sunstein, C. R. (2005b). Moral heuristics. *Behavioral and Brain Sciences, 28*(4), 531–541.

Talhelm, T., Haidt, J., Oishi, S., Zhang, X., Miao, F. F., & Chen, S. (2015). Liberals think more analytically (more "WEIRD") than conservatives. *Personality and Social Psychology Bulletin, 41*(2), 250–267.

Thaler, R. (1980). Toward a positive theory of consumer choice. *Journal of Economic Behavior & Organization, 1*(1), 39–60.

Thaler, R. (2015). *Misbehaving: The making of behavioral economics.* W. W. Norton & Company.

Thompson, V. A., & Johnson, S. C. (2014). Conflict, metacognition, and analytic thinking. *Thinking & Reasoning, 20*(2), 215–244.

Thompson, V. A., Turner, J. A. P., & Pennycook, G. (2011). Intuition, reason, and metacognition. *Cognitive Psychology, 63*(3), 107–140.

Tiberius, V. (2014). *Moral psychology: A contemporary introduction.* Routledge.

Toplak, M. E., West, R. F., & Stanovich, K. E. (2014). Assessing miserly information processing: An expansion of the cognitive reflection test. *Thinking & Reasoning, 20*(2), 147–168.

Trémolière, B., & De Neys, W. (2014). When intuitions are helpful: Prior beliefs can support reasoning in the bat-and-ball problem. *Journal of Cognitive Psychology, 26*(4), 486–490.

Tversky, A., & Kahneman, D. (1973). Availability: A heuristic for judging frequency and probability. *Cognitive Psychology, 5*(2), 207–232.

van Berkel, L., Crandall, C. S., Eidelman, S., & Blanchar, J. C. (2015). Hierarchy, dominance, and deliberation: Egalitarian values require mental effort. *Personality and Social Psychology Bulletin, 41*(9), 1207–1222.

Västfjäll, D., Slovic, P., & Mayorga, M. (2015). Pseudoinefficacy: Negative feelings from children who cannot be helped reduce warm glow for children who can be helped. *Frontiers of Psychology, 6*(616).

Västfjäll, D., Slovic, P., Mayorga, M., & Peters, E. (2014). Compassion fade: Affect and charity are greatest for a single child in need. *PLoS One, 9*(6), e100115.

Wegner, D. (2002). *The illusion of conscious will.* Cambridge, MA, MIT Press.

Widerquist, K., & McCall, G. S. (2017). *Prehistoric myths in modern political philosophy.* Edinburgh University Press.

Wilson, T. D. (2002). *Strangers to ourselves: Discovering the adaptive unconscious.* Cambridge, MA, Belknap Press of Harvard University Press.

Wilson, T. D., Dunn, D. S. et al. (1989). "Introspection, Attitude Change, and Attitude-Behavior Consistency: The Disruptive Effects of Explaining Why We Feel the Way We Do." In: L. Berkowitz (ed.). *Advances in experimental social psychology.* San Diego, Academic Press: 287–343.

Wilson, T. D., & Schooler, J. W. (1991). Thinking too much: Introspection can reduce the quality of preferences and decisions. *Journal of Personality and Social Psychology, 60*(2), 181–192.

Wojcik, S. P., Hovasapian, A., Graham, J., Motyl, M., & Ditto, P. H. (2015). Conservatives report, but liberals display, greater happiness. *Science, 347*(6227), 1243–1246.

Wood, T., & Porter, E. (2016). "The Elusive Backfire Effect: Mass Attitudes' Steadfast Factual Adherence." Manuscript.

Wright, J. C., & Baril, G. (2011). The role of cognitive resources in determining our moral intuitions: Are we all liberals at heart? *Journal of Experimental Social Psychology, 47*(5), 1007–1012.

Yilmaz, O., & Saribay, S. A. (2017). Activating analytic thinking enhances the value given to individualizing moral foundations. *Cognition, 165*, 88–96.

Zwolinski, M. (2008). The ethics of price gouging. *Business Ethics Quarterly, 18*(3), 347–378.

# Index

Printed in the United States
by Baker & Taylor Publisher Services